ZENEIDA AND OTHER PLAYS

Borgo Press Books by FRANK J. MORLOCK

The Chevalier d'Éon and Other Short Farces (Editor)
Chuzzlewit
Congreve's Comedy of Manners
Crime and Punishment
Cyrano and Molière: Five Plays by or About Molière (Editor)
Falstaff (with William Shakespeare, John Dennis, and William Kendrick)
Fathers and Sons
The Idiot
Jurgen
Justine
Lord Jim
The Madwoman of Beresina and Other Napoleonic Plays (Editor)
Notes from the Underground
Oblomov
Old Creole Days
Outrageous Women: Lady Macbeth and Other French Plays (Editor)
Peter and Alexis
The Princess Casamassima
A Raw Youth
The Stendhal Hamlet Scenarios and Other Shakespearean Shorts from the French (Editor)
Two Voltairean Plays: The Triumvirate; and, Comedy at Ferney (editor)
The Widow's Husband; and, Porthos in Search of an Outfit: Two Dumasian Comedies (Editor)
Zeneida and The Follies of Love and The Cat Who Changed into a Woman: Three Plays (Editor)

ZENEIDA & THE FOLLIES OF LOVE

& THE CAT WHO CHANGED INTO A WOMAN: THREE PLAYS

FRANK J. MORLOCK, EDITOR

THE BORGO PRESS
MMXIII

ZENEIDA & THE FOLLIES OF LOVE

Copyright © 1987, 2006, 2013 by Frank J. Morlock

FIRST EDITION

Published by Wildside Press LLC

www.wildsidebooks.com

DEDICATION

For Carmen Martínez

CONTENTS

ZENEIDA 9
CAST OF CHARACTERS 10
THE PLAY 10
THE FOLLIES OF LOVE 65
CAST OF CHARACTERS 66
ACT I 67
ACT II 93
ACT III 121
THE CAT WHO CHANGED INTO A WOMAN 143
CAST OF CHARACTERS 144
THE PLAY 145
ABOUT THE EDITOR 212

ZENEIDA
by Louis de Cuhasac

CAST OF CHARACTERS

THE FAIRY

ZENEIDA

DAGNY (originally Gnidie)

ROLAND (originally Olinde)

THE PLAY

THE FAIRY:

There you are, Zeneida, a bit compensated
For the retreat in which you are living in here.
But where did this new care arise from
In which your soul seems plunged?
I've transported you to places embellished
By Art, Nature, and the Graces,
And yet in your softened eyes
I am finding traces of an intense sorrow?
You are sighing? Admit frankly
That the fest for you had some pleasure.
The ball amused you; this Palace bores you.

ZENEIDA:

Lovable Fairy, it is true; all these new objects
Have some attractions for me,
But I've followed you first of all.

FAIRY:

I admit it; but sighing,
You were looking, leaving
With eyes of desire and envy
This ball so attractive for you.
Zeneida, I see your soul completely naked.
I am reading dangerous secrets in it
Which are escaping from your eyes
And that have struck my sight.

ZENEIDA:

(worried) O Heaven! What have I done so wrong?
I saw the ball with you,
On the bench where you placed me.
That's all I think.

THE FAIRY:

And this air of anger
That you displayed when I forced you
To watch this jealous mask.
Who despite the hurrying crowd
Of the curious who swarmed around us,

And yet more despite yourself,
To the glances you kept hidden?

ZENEIDA:

It's true, you annoyed me—
And the heat of the ball—

THE FAIRY:

You didn't feel it anymore
When, for that reason, I wanted to disappear.

ZENEIDA:

(excitedly) But why these superfluous cares?
Why are you refusing to let me know?
I owe you everything; and I no longer see
Those from whom heaven gave me birth.
It's through your power that I hold my attractions.
Can I cherish your benefits too much?
To decorate myself with them—that's recognizing them

THE FAIRY:

And your prayers would be satisfied
If you had made this recognition known
To this young stranger whose amiable presence—

ZENEIDA:

Oh! Madame, I know his name.

FAIRY:

Does he know yours and in what fashion
My tenderness has taken care to raise your childhood?

ZENEIDA:

He asked me everything, but with so much intensity—

FAIRY:

That you told him everything.

ZENEIDA:

Roland is so pressing,
He prayed to me so tenderly
That he vanquished my resistance.
But perhaps I did wrong.

FAIRY:

Then, to your eyes,
He's very interesting, very lovable?

ZENEIDA:

Madame, he is charming.

FAIRY:

Perhaps, around here,
He's revealed himself on a favorable day,
And if you were to know him better—

ZENEIDA:

No question he would please me more.
Many others have spoken to me, but their air, their language,
Their gayety, their tone and their efforts,
Their rush to please me,
Have done exactly the contrary.
They had too much wit—

FAIRY:

Roland has some, at least?

ZENEIDA:

To be honest, I don't know.
But, with him, I felt he had.
When I was speaking, his eyes made me see
That he was experiencing an extreme pleasure.
In truth all the others
Appeared to me to be satisfied with themselves.
He alone was only for me.

FAIRY:

I see it, it is time to break silence.
Your fate is going to reveal itself.
With prudence one can often
Correct the malign influence of the stars,
Avoid it, or repair it,
And if your happiness is not in my power,
I must at least enlighten you.
In a moment Roland is going to appear.

ZENEIDA:

What, Madame, in this palace?
What, I will see him right away?

FAIRY:

He will see you too soon, perhaps.
Zeneida, you are unaware
That this inclination which drags you toward him,
This cruel pain in leaving him,
This pleasure in seeing him when you imagine him,
Is the first access of an intense passion
That your tender and naive soul
Will burn with so long as you live.
In your heart, Love, in a word, has just burgeoned.

ZENEIDA:

Love! Could it be a misfortune? Is it a blessing? I'm

unaware.

FAIRY:

It can make your life miserable.

ZENEIDA:

Truly, my terror is extreme.

FAIRY:

But if your Roland loves you
With a love that lasts forever,
Count on a supreme happiness
Whose course nothing can alter.

ZENEIDA:

Why, in that case, love is not so formidable?

FAIRY:

I see him. You know that you are lovable.

ZENEIDA:

Eh, but. Perhaps Roland will love me.

FAIRY:

Since he's a man, he will change.

ZENEIDA:

Ah! I don't doubt it, I will be unfortunate.
I'll never know how to change.

FAIRY:

That's not all. A rigorous law
Threatens your life with a danger
Which all my art cannot free you from.
There are secrets that I must no longer hide
From when you received life,
I rushed; I saw you with the eyes of a mother.
And too blind in my love,
From a fatal prejudice following extravagance,
Thinking like a woman at last, I believed that beauty
Was the blessing par excellence,
The supreme felicity.
So I exhausted my power
To dower you with all the vain attractions
Of the most brilliant face.
All my art served to embellish your features.
I abandoned the rest to nature.
The fairy Urganda appeared at this moment.
My soul was worried by her appearance.
Her threatening looks announced her wrath to me.
She said to me in a feverish tone:
You ought to know that one day they must love her.—
With my respect I thought to disarm her.
She approached you, touched you, embraced you.
I was unaware if it was favor or disgrace

That Urganda poured over you,
But by the ills with which she threatened you,
I must judge her wrath.

ZENEIDA:

I am trembling. Finish, I beg you.
What ills must I worry about?
Roland, ought I to fear for your life?

FAIRY:

Here are her own words; I am going to repeat them.
Zeneida, you'll be beautiful.
But fear love; if one day it wounds your heart,
Your beauty will become ugliness,
If you don't please your lover without it.

ZENEIDA:

O Heaven! I will become—?

FAIRY:

Yes, ugly enough to frighten.

ZENEIDA:

Roland will find me ugly!
Ah! Don't let him come; I would die of sorrow.

FAIRY:

To the power of the Fairy, mine has to give in
And since Roland has pleased you,
You must see him, and if it's possible, please him
As Urganda has decided.
Of your love, especially be careful to be silent.
For the plan I've conceived,
That's the capital point.

ZENEIDA:

And the most difficult.
For if he loves me, could I hide it from him?
I don't know how to dissimulate to that degree.
My mouth will keep silent uselessly
And, despite me, my eyes will know how to speak.

FAIRY:

And ugliness.

ZENEIDA:

You are making me tremble.
Instruct me:
what must I do?

FAIRY:

Well, your situation embarrasses me.
Men are so dangerous,

It's so difficult to find a sincere one!
The way he appears to our eyes
Is only a trickster seeking to please
With specious outsides.
Caprice rules their prayers
Or vanity causes their birth.
Flighty, Proud, Ungrateful,
The heart prefers at pleasure to be happy,
The false honor of appearing so
And the most modest of them all
On this article is the fop.

ZENEIDA:

What is it to think so falsely?
Ah! If I enjoyed the pleasure of being loved
I would know how to shut in this important secret
Between my heart and my lover.
But alas, my startled soul
Must deliver itself to other cares.
No, I must no longer hope
For a happiness that would have charmed me.

FAIRY:

Why not? There's a way.

ZENEIDA:

(excitedly) A way?

FAIRY:

(malignly) I would have some hope,
If by chance, Roland indeed was thinking
The thing would be rare and pass appearance.
Still, it's possible.
Sometimes I've seen propitious nature,
By a lucky caprice,
Make miracles when playing.

ZENEIDA:

If he was indeed thinking—

FAIRY:

He hasn't seen you.
A mask has veiled your features,
And yet is his soul disturbed?
By his farewells, by his regrets,
I've seen how much for you it was prepared.

ZENEIDA:

I also really noticed it,
Anyway, what he told me, quite hushed,
—All men don't have this tender and timid air.

FAIRY:

They find so many lures to deceive us,
What pleases is the only thing that guides them.

ZENEIDA:

Still, if there's one who isn't false,
I'd wager that Roland isn't.

FAIRY:

Well, let's test his tenderness.
Beware of discovering to him
How much your heart is interested,
And still to obey
The absolute orders of Urganda
Hide your beauty from your lover.
Try to enflame him as she directed.
Let the mask firmly
Conceal from his glances.

(Enter Dagny in casual dress.)

DAGNY:

Zeneida. (to Fairy) Ah! Madame,
Pardon me. I didn't see you.

FAIRY:

What's the matter with you?
Where's this embarrassment come from?

DAGNY:

Nothing is equal to the trouble of my soul.

I saw him in the gardens. His air is enchanting,
God! How pretty his face is.
Perhaps you accuse me of madness,
But I saw him, I tell you, and I really believe my heart
   over it.

FAIRY:

Who did you see, Dagny?

DAGNY:

A charming young man. Must I tell you again?

ZENEIDA:

(to Fairy) Ah! It's him; I cannot doubt it.

FAIRY:

(to Dagny) And did he notice you?

DAGNY:

I really flatter myself that he saw me.
But I wouldn't dare be sure of it.
He was still far off. I was so casual.
I fled to go gussy up,
If I had been better fixed—

FAIRY:

I understand; you would have taken great care to show yourself?

DAGNY:

To see him again I'm going to prepare myself.
(to Zeneida) Suppose I were to wear the dress and hairdo
That I wore when they made my portrait?
I prefer that attire.
(to fairy) It's to your taste, and I'll get ready right away.
G'bye, I'm rushing to get dressed.

(Dagny leaves.)

ZENEIDA:

(very excitedly) Ah! Madame she will please him.
Forbid her—

FAIRY:

What, my daughter, already
A jealous care disturbs you?
Reassure yourself.

ZENEIDA:

(with scorn) Without this importunate mask,
Or if Dagny had one,

I wouldn't suspect her.
But she is so beautiful; she will want to please him.
Roland will see her allures.

FAIRY:

What matter if he loves you?

ZENEIDA:

He can change for her.

FAIRY:

In that case, to Urganda's orders
It is easy to be faithful.
You will be beautiful, at least.

ZENEIDA:

And if he doesn't love me,
What do I care about being beautiful?

FAIRY:

I hear some noise.

ZENEIDA:

My heart's beating. It's him.
(to Fairy) What! You are abandoning me.

FAIRY:

He's coming. Be prudent.
You hear.

(Exit Fairy.)

ZENEIDA:

(alone, putting on her mask) Alas! Today I feared
To see him too late for my fervor's taste;
And now, uneasy, trembling—

(Enter Roland.)

ROLAND:

I see her again! Zeneida, it's you?
How flattering this moment is to my passion.
I was sighing after a blessing so sweet
And I felt my soul flying towards you.

ZENEIDA:

(aside) I feel all he's saying.

ROLAND:

But what! For the reward of a passion so tender
You seem not to hear me.

ZENEIDA:

(as she turns) Pardon me, I am listening to you.

ROLAND:

What do I see? O Heaven! That insupportable mask
Again hiding your attractions from my love!
Eh! Am I never to see you
Except under an impenetrable veil?

ZENEIDA:

Alas! I am annoyed by it and I would wish
For you to see me with less mystery,
But—

ROLAND:

Well?

ZENEIDA:

Oh! I know how to shut up.

(aside, making a gesture to leave)
Got to get away from him; I will ruin myself.
I feel I'm listening to him with too much pleasure.

(to Roland)

Roland, leave me alone. With a feigned ardor,

No question, you intend to deceive me.

ROLAND:

Me, deceive you?

ZENEIDA:

The Fairy, luckily,
Had the care to instruct me.
This curious desire, this flattering talk,
Would have been able to seduce me without her.
One more time, Roland, leave me alone.
I know that the most honest man
Is ungrateful, perfidious or flighty,
And you won't keep your faith with me.

ROLAND:

Ah, Zeneida, what talk!
Such a suspicion overwhelms me with sorrow.
At my age you know few men
But believe in my testimony.
They've depicted to you too starkly.
Vices are not their sole appanage.
Some virtues speak in their favor
And confidence at least, must be their share.
If I judge of them by my heart,
Deign to do me justice!
Tear off this odious mask;
Be propitious to my desires.

Zeneida, these features will fulfill my prayers
If they were offered to my eyes.
Your refusal is my torture.
Is it from hate, or from caprice,
That you are making me wretched?

ZENEIDA:

(placing her hand on her mask, aside)

I am giving in to his extreme ardor.

(pulling back her hand hurriedly)

If he's deceiving me! If he's deceiving himself!

ROLAND:

What do I see? This flattering concern—
Does it speak to you in my favor?

ZENEIDA:

(aside) I don't know where I am,
And my reason is forgetting itself.
Ah, if he were to observe it! Shall I betray myself?
(to Roland) At least, I do not love you.

ROLAND:

I see that only too well, ingrate.
I displease you, you reject my cares!

ZENEIDA:

What are you saying?

ROLAND:

My despair flatters you.
You make me feel it too much,
Yes, you hate me. Well, I must flee you.

ZENEIDA:

Why, I don't hate you; I know that very well, perhaps.

ROLAND:

Then let yourself be softened by my love.

ZENEIDA:

(aside) My heart is no longer the master of my secret.
(to Roland) Roland, do you love me?

ROLAND:

Can you doubt it?

ZENEIDA:

Prove it to me by your obedience.

ROLAND:

Command, I can attempt anything.

ZENEIDA:

I must hide my features and keep silent.

ROLAND:

Ah! Zeneida, would you
Despair a heart that adores you?
Why veil your sweetest attractions,
Why this mask that I abhor,
When love alone is in cahoots with us?

(he goes to his knees)

I am going to die at your knees
If I don't obtain the favor that I implore.

ZENEIDA:

Ah!

ROLAND:

Is this sigh favorable to my passion?
Reveal yourself and I am happy,
Give in to my impatience.

ZENEIDA:

(aside) Alas! They are all so pressing.
What help can prudence be against them?

ROLAND:

My dear Zeneida!

ZENEIDA:

Roland! Ah, what moments!

ROLAND:

Let them be sweet for me without your resistance!

(he rises to remove her mask)

Ah! Allow me—

ZENEIDA:

No, I forbid it!

ROLAND:

(continuing) O Heaven! What unjust prohibition.

ZENEIDA:

(defending herself) Roland, get over it.

ROLAND:

(with more passion) My passion is too ardent
For this effort of obedience.
I am dying with the exaltation I feel.

ZENEIDA:

That's enough of it, stop, or fear my wrath.

ROLAND:

What? I can't be allowed?

ZENEIDA:

I have the courage necessary
To hide myself and remain silent
When you stop being submissive.

ROLAND:

You wish it; despite myself I obey,
But I have a notion of the depths of this mystery.

ZENEIDA:

And what notion do you have?

ROLAND:

(aside) Let's excite her vanity.

ZENEIDA:

Speak.

ROLAND:

Since I am forced to be sincere,
One doesn't hide to this degree when one has wherewithal to please.

ZENEIDA:

(stung) So you predict very ill of my beauty?

ROLAND:

But without trusting it. I suspect.

ZENEIDA:

Fine, I understand that sincerity.
(aside) Ah, if I dared. But, no, the means he's giving me,
Let's profit by it to sound the recesses of his heart.
(aloud) Your suspicion is only too true.
Roland, you are forcing my candor to this confession.
It is very true, to my misfortune,
That my features are not agreeable at all.
That's my whole secret.

ROLAND:

No, I don't believe you.
My heart is speaking to me; it depicts your attractions
And to it alone am I listening.

ZENEIDA:

Your suspicions—

ROLAND:

I was hoping to conquer your refusal
By interesting your glory.

ZENEIDA:

They are founded.

ROLAND:

Let's not speak of it anymore;
They were feigned; forget about them.

ZENEIDA:

There's nothing offensive in them for me.
Beauty would render me a bit vain.
It's a flower that flatters and pleases for a moment
But which perishes almost in being born
And my ugliness doesn't trouble me.

ROLAND:

Ah! Vain for you to say it and I don't believe you.
No, the most honest woman
Was never secure to this degree;
The ugliest believe the contrary.
You are beautiful and very sure of pleasing;
Your mirror has told you so often.
If it was necessary, I'd swear to it
From your talk alone.

ZENEIDA:

Your obstinacy annoys me
I know myself, apparently,
And I tell you I am ugly.
No more arguing, or I'll get angry.

ROLAND:

You are forcing me to it; well, I shall believe you.

ZENEIDA:

(aside) You believe me! He thinks it, the traitor!

(to Roland, timidly)

And this love which gave birth,
A vain phantom of beauty
By which your heart was flattered
Before knowing me very well,

Apparently is going to vanish
With the mistake which enchanted you?

ROLAND:

No. My love will always be the same.
You want in vain to alarm me.
Be ugly. I love you
And I won't ever stop loving you.

ZENEIDA:

What! If I were extremely ugly?

ROLAND:

But you are not.

ZENEIDA:

Yet, if I were?

ROLAND:

I feel that I would love you.

ZENEIDA:

(aside) I am enjoying a supreme happiness.
(to Roland) Roland, is it really true? you are not deceiving yourself?
Is a man capable of such an effort?

ROLAND:

Even if the mask be favorable,
To my eyes you lend it attractions,
Even if it covers a lovable face,
I feel myself seized near you
By an irresistible inclination
About you I feel myself stopped.
The sound of your voice, this ingeniousness,
Your graces, your wit, this agreeable smile,
These glances which, despite this mask overwhelm me,
Make me experience their conquering allures,
Even without beauty, will render you adorable.

ZENEIDA:

That's enough; I am in a ravishing state,
Roland. O heaven! What is my joy?
I am going to find the Fairy:
I have to see her.
Roland, wait a moment.

ROLAND:

Ah! let me follow you.

ZENEIDA:

No: stay; I'll be back in a minute.

(Zeneida prepares to leave.)

ZENEIDA:

(at the back of the stage, before leaving)

Don't go away, at least. (exit)

ROLAND:

(alone) Ah what torture!
I don't know how to live in this situation.
Is it really true that she has told her secret?
After all, what's it matter? I adore her.
Since she loves me in her turn,
I will make her keep her mask on all day.
But someone's coming. Is this Venus or Flora?

(Enter Dagny.)

DAGNY:

(aside) It's himself; let's approach,
Let him be able to see my features.

ROLAND:

(aside) What a get-up, and what allures!
How perfectly it suits her face!
Zeneida without these trimmings
Pleases me even more.
(to Dagny) One must experience the sweetest happiness here
Where one is meeting all the pleasures together

If the diverse objects that the fairy puts together
Are all as charming as you.

DAGNY:

You find me nice, then? Ah, how lovable a man is!
Do you know that in this retreat
No one has yet told me the like?

ROLAND:

Then there are few gallants?

DAGNY:

And truly very few.
The Fairy only has women in her court.
They control me without cease;
Any one thing aggravates their envious spirits.
And something about me always injures them.
I return them tenderness for tenderness
And I judge them strictly.
On that point I have no scruples.
By their face or their humor
I see them all, luckily,
Stupids, uglies or laughables,
And I hate them with all my heart.

ROLAND:

(aside) Charming natural! She resembles others;
What's more, she's of good faith.

(to Dagny) But tell me, in this palace
Don't you see charms other than your own?
Isn't there some object you can praise?

DAGNY:

But I see so many people there, and besides I'm good.
I am still constrained to admit
That I don't meet anyone
Whose faults don't strike my glances.
For example, the Fairy is unjust, imperious;
At all times, for us she lacks concern.
Floride, as she boasts, is beautiful, generous,
And her figure majestic,
At first approach dazzling,
But to see her closer, soon the charm flees.
Outside sharpness conceals a proud soul.
Her strong tone shocks, aggravates.
She is mean, ungrateful, disdainful.
In short, impertinence makes her ugly
Like the others. Nature vainly
Embellishes her with a thousand attractions.
They mar their face
Through the defect of their wit.

ROLAND:

Your brush doesn't flatter.

DAGNY:

It is less malign than sincere
I pine after the original.

ROLAND:

(timidly) And Zeneida?

DAGNY:

Eh, why is right to please,
I found her nice enough, her wit is so-so,
And besides, she has a very nice character.

ROLAND:

(aside) She's ugly, the thing is clear,
Since she hasn't spoken ill of her.
(to Dagny) Then you love her a lot?

DAGNY:

Yes, everybody loves her.

ROLAND:

(aside) Now there at least my taste is justified.

DAGNY:

The fairy has moments of friendship for the two of us.

Her kindness, in that case, is extreme.
To paint and knit are her amusements.
In one of her moments
She wanted to do my portrait herself.
It's really pretty. The decorations especially,
I will let you see it. I think you have good taste.
Well, in this palace, be it base jealousy,
Or lack of discrimination,
Only Zeneida, yes, only she alone,
Was just enough, or even polite enough
To find me even more pretty
Than this portrait that was boasted of.

ROLAND:

No question, she was fair like a good friend,
And however little it may resemble—

DAGNY:

Oh! it's not a bad resemblance.
I told you, you will see it;
Like her you will judge it.
We will meet some other time together.
But I beg you, are you alone here?
We do not like going around except in company.
Apparently men go this way?
Where are your companions?

(aside)

He finds me pretty,
They will have good eyes, too.

ROLAND:

(aside) Ah! what depths of flirtatiousness.
(to Dagny) I came alone.

DAGNY:

What, alone in this place?

ROLAND:

Yes, alone. Does that mortify you?
For the glory of your attractions,
There's little except my vote.

DAGNY:

I don't say that; but still, I would like—

ROLAND:

To force everybody to render you homage?

DAGNY:

The Fairy's approaching; goodbye.
I am leaving you with regret.
(aside) I see he finds me charming.
Let's run to Zeneida to share this secret;

I intend to give her my confidence.

(Exit Dagny.)

ROLAND:

(alone) How different Zeneida is.
Qualities of heart are alone true treasures;
Without them beauty ceases to be attractive.

FAIRY:

(entering) I've retained my distraction for a while.
I want to see him myself, before she exposes herself—

ROLAND:

You know the cause of my pain.
Doubtless the power of your art allows you
To read my heart like myself.
You see my intense love.
I am expecting my blessing from you and Zeneida.

FAIRY:

I transported you into this pleasant abode
With the plan of joining the two of you.
Hope for everything if you feel
The flames of a durable love.

ROLAND:

What! I could flatter myself with being happy?

FAIRY:

I am unaware if her soul is interested in you.
It suffices for me, to unite you,
To know of your tenderness.
Zeneida is well born and will know to obey me.

ROLAND:

Ah! Madame, what are you daring to say?
Her hand is the sole blessing my soul desires.
But from your power, were I to perish,
I don't expect the happiness to which I aspire.
It's only from her heart that I wish to obtain it.

FAIRY:

I love to find this delicacy in you.
But examine yourself. Tell me frankly.
Zeneida is youthful,
Her graces, wit, lots of feeling,
But that's all, and her ugliness is such—

ROLAND:

So she's ugly—absolutely?

THE FAIRY:

Yes, I'd be painting an unfaithful portrait
If I pictured her otherwise.

ROLAND:

With such beautiful eyes, can she not be beautiful?

FAIRY:

But from where does this astonishment come?
On this point she should have spoken to you without mystery.

ROLAND:

Ah! I don't know. My love was flattering itself.
I hoped she was deceiving me
About her ugliness. Are you really sincere?

FAIRY:

No question, you will be revolted.

ROLAND:

No. Her graces, her character,
Have seduced me. I am enchanted by 'em
And, at bottom, lasting beauty
Is nothing else than the gift of pleasing.
Let her appear then, and before your eyes,

I am going to consecrate my love and my life to her.

FAIRY:

If you were to see her before—Yes, that would be much
  better.
I have her portrait with me.

ROLAND:

(with eagerness) Madame, I beg you,
Permit me to see it a moment.

FAIRY:

(aside) Heavens. He's going to endure a cruel test,
But the happiness of both of them depends on it.

ROLAND:

(almost terrified) What do I see? O heaven!
Is this really she?

FAIRY:

It flatters her a bit, but a prudent painter
Must sometimes embellish his model.

ROLAND:

And this portrait you say, is flattering?

FAIRY:

No question. Eh, what! Now there you are, already
    disheartened?
A mortal frigidity succeeds your distractions?

ROLAND:

I must admit I thought her less ugly.

FAIRY:

I indeed told you; her features are odious.
Admit now that this very tender passion
Is already distant.

ROLAND:

There are still her eyes
And all her features to take it well
Are not bad.

FAIRY:

But the ensemble is frightful.

ROLAND:

Frightful! That's too much. Her ugliness—

FAIRY:

Is extreme.

ROLAND:

There's nothing shocking in the depths of it.

FAIRY:

What? You find—

ROLAND:

And I even observe

Something touching.

Examine, madam, this mouth.

FAIRY:

The mouth's all right.

ROLAND:

But, I tell you, very fine.
She has this touching smile
And nothing can compare to hers.

(Enter Zeneida, still masked, with Dagny.)

ZENEIDA:

Madame, he was deceiving me; he adores Dagny.
(to Roland) Ah! There you are!

DAGNY:

(to Roland) You find me pretty?
Isn't it true you said that?

ROLAND:

(coldly) I told you that and I repeat it.

ZENEIDA:

(to Fairy) Right in front of my eyes he is betraying me!

ROLAND:

(to Dagny) No question, your face is perfect.
Good taste alone suffices to find it so.

DAGNY:

(to Zeneida) Well, darling, did I deceive you?
Go, I am sure of pleasing
And I think my attractions less than your spite.

FAIRY:

(to Zeneida) What, you are weeping?

ZENEIDA:

I am desperate.

ROLAND:

Zeneida!

ZENEIDA:

How I hate her!

FAIRY:

Here all were living in peace.
A young man appears, war is declared.

ROLAND:

You can suspect?

ZENEIDA:

Oh! I know well enough.
Don't hope to deceive me again.
But what is this portrait? Doubtless it's his.

ROLAND:

It's the portrait of the one I adore.

DAGNY:

(in a reserved manner) What! Madam gave you mine so soon?

ROLAND:

(to Dagny) You are mistaken and this is of someone else.

DAGNY:

He's raving and I don't understand a thing.

ZENEIDA:

But this portrait, whose is it?

ROLAND:

It's yours.

ZENEIDA:

(taking the portrait) Mine? I want to see it.

FAIRY:

It's going to frighten her.

ZENEIDA:

(casting the portrait away) O Heaven! What is this

imposture?
It's truly a monster of ugliness.

ROLAND:

Why, not at all.

ZENEIDA:

It's she, I am sure of it,
Who played me this bloody trick.
She finds her score by making me ugly.

DAGNY:

I please him without cheating
And I triumph by revealing myself.

ROLAND:

Finally, this portrait, I beg you,
What's so displeasing about it?

(tenderly)

It's yours and my ravished soul—

ZENEIDA:

Stop this joking.

ROLAND:

I am not joking.

ZENEIDA:

What a shocking proceeding.

ROLAND:

(to the Fairy) Madame, explain then.

FAIRY:

(laughing) On this important point
We won't hear any joking.

ZENEIDA:

I am outraged, and my scorn—

FAIRY:

(to Zeneida) Calm down. (aside) Her rage is amusing.

DAGNY:

(ironically) What's she upset about? He found her charming.

ROLAND:

(annoyed, showing the portrait) Why, it's incontrovertibly her.

ZENEIDA:

He's outraging me with every word he says. (to Roland) That's too much. I loved you.

FAIRY:

Remember Urganda.

ZENEIDA:

It's no longer anything that I apprehend.
Yes, I loved you.

ROLAND:

Is this you that I hear?

ZENEIDA:

But his pride, your perfidy,
Is changing my tender feelings for you into hate.

ROLAND:

Rather tear out my life.

ZENEIDA:

To avenge myself at the same time

For your frivolity, for her coquetry,
Look, ingrate, see if Dagny
Ought to have won out over me.

(Zeneida unmasks.)

ROLAND:

What do I see? O Heaven!

ZENEIDA:

No question Urganda has punished me.
I am horrible, he recoils in fright.

(to the Fairy)

Madame, am I really frightful?

FAIRY:

(laughing) A bit less than your portrait.

ROLAND:

Is this a flattering illusion?
I've seen nothing so perfect.

DAGNY:

The dummy! In my presence he boasts of Zeneida!

ZENEIDA:

What, I am not ugly?

ROLAND:

Ah! The day is less beautiful.
Why, these attractions, to the love that guides me,
Are not loaning a new passion—

ZENEIDA:

(to the fairy) I love him, I told him, and I am still beautiful!
Then, he isn't perfidious?

FAIRY:

(laughing) Eh, why he maintains it.

DAGNY:

It is now what he will become.

ROLAND:

(to Zeneida) Madame is the witness to my faithful passion.

ZENEIDA:

But Dagny?

ROLAND:

It is certain that I love only you.
I swear it to you at your knees.

DAGNY:

What, you change like this? Because you loved me.

ROLAND:

One can praise in good faith
Without the soul being enflamed.

DAGNY:

(leaving) Ah! the fickle!

ZENEIDA:

And the portrait?

FAIRY:

It's I
Who wanted to test him. Stop being alarmed.
Happily, my efforts succeeded.

ROLAND:

Eh! Why test me like that?
What? Can't your art let you read in hearts?

FAIRY:

My art is submissive to Love.
But let's not think anymore on this day
Except of crowning the flames that inspire you.

ZENEIDA:

Then I can, without trembling, love you, tell you so?

ROLAND:

I adore you, and your divine allures
Are new blessings that I admire,
But I didn't desire them.

FAIRY:

(to Roland) Your soul surrendered to lasting charms.
Those that offer beauty are really less desirable,
And steal off with the years.
A solid happiness will be your share,
And Love, guiding the feelings of your hearts,
Will triumph until the decline of age
And habit and time.
Let these parts embellish themselves at my voice.
You who live happily under my directives,
Come, reassemble, let your songs applaud
The happiness of these tender lovers.

(Genies, the troupe of young girls raised in the palace run in dancing.)

A SERVING GIRL OF THE FAIRY:

CANTATAILLE

Love animates these abodes.
Already the sound of our bag pipes
Feel the pleasures with which your heart rejoices!
This charming God, is going to spread through the air
An agreeable and sweet languor.
The breath of Zephyrs embellish each flower.
The warbling of nightingales is more tender.
All express your happiness.

(They dance.)

A SERVING GIRL OF THE FAIRY:

ARIETE

Young beauties, all rush to please you.
But beware the ravages of time.
Wit, heart, the charm of talents
Suspend it's fickle course
And alone can prolong your beautiful years.

VAUDEVILLE

I.

When beauty alone seduces
One loves for a day, then one languishes.
Love steals off, one is detested

But when heart gives way to talent
To character, to feelings
Time alone flees, and love remains.

II.

Against his revolted parents
Damon, by an idol enchanted,
Is going to utter a funereal yes.
But the charms that seduced him
Soon withered, Love flees
And unluckily, the woman remains.

III.

—"At Court I have good friends
I am sure of Lord Damis"
Said a modest financier
Damis exhausted his credit
The was eclipsed, the friend fled
And unluckily the debt remains.

IV.

They believe in triumphing over a lover
They resist him, they defend themselves
But it's vain that they struggle
Love smiles at these battles
The moment comes, reason flees
And the obstinate gallant remains.

V.

When the theatre gets drowsy
The play fails, the author flees
The envious laugh, and the actor fumes
But when the public applauds
The author shows himself, the actor laughs
The envious flee, the play remains.

(Counter-Dance.)

CURTAIN

THE FOLLIES OF LOVE
by Jean-François Regnard

CAST OF CHARACTERS

Albert

Worthy

Arabella

Jenny

Scratch

ACT I

Outside a country house at the end of the seventeenth century. Dawn.

Jenny enters following Arabella.

Jenny

Why, when every one else is sleeping, what demon, if you please, tugs you by the ear and makes you go up and out so early?

Arabella

Peace, shut up, speak low. You know my plan. Worthy has come back.

Jenny

Worthy?

Arabella (romantically)

From France!

Jenny

How do you know that, Madame, I beg to ask?

Arabella

I believed he'd make an appearance hereabouts more with my heart than my eyes.

Jenny

I am only astonished that you've avoided the watchful Uncle Albert. My word, here is a guide more excellent than love.

Arabella

I was at my window waiting for the day. Then, someone came. Seeing the door open, I seized the opportunity offered by the occasion—more to take the air than to flatter my hopes that Mr. Worthy would be attracted here just to see me.

Jenny

There's no need for you to worry. It's understandable that the poor boy would fall all over himself to see you. He comes tonight, and at daybreak, you wait for him—just to flatter his love. You lose little time. But, what, if by chance, Albert, your tutor, who is jealous by nature, should find us? What would you say to him?

Arabella (with determination)

I intend to free myself from the jealous fool. I have languished too long under his cruel domain. I'm taking off the mask, so he can see how little regard I have for him, and how I intend to live from now on—and how much I hate him!

Jenny

May heaven assist you in this praiseworthy plan! As for me, I'd rather serve the devil, yes, the devil. At least when he held his Sabbath, I would have some rest. But, in my state, evening, morning, day or night, I have no peace. I'll have a breakdown soon. He scolds and grinds his teeth the live long day.— Do this, do that, come, go, go upstairs, go downstairs, close the door and window. Prevent, if you can, anyone from appearing.— He stops, he worries, he runs around without knowing where. All night he prowls like a frenzied wolf. He doesn't permit us to close our eyes. As for him, when he sleeps, one eye's shut, the other's watching. He never laughed in his life. He's jealous, stupid, brutal to the extreme, miserly, hard, peevish. I'd prefer to beg for my bread, from door to door, than to serve a master like this any longer. In short, I don't like him.

Arabella

Henceforth, Jenny, all our troubles are over. How my

Worthy differs from the portrait you paint. From my most tender years, nursed by his own mother, our hearts were leagued in sympathy. And love grew by the most charming means, finally united again by mutual oaths. Although suffering from this frightful constraint for some time, which annoys and overwhelms me, I am a woman who will take violent action! Dressed like a man, a knight errant, I will free myself from Albert and his harsh tyranny. I am going to run away and seek adventures.

Jenny

Oh, there are adventures enough to be found without going so far away. I can warn you that you will find enough of them.

Arabella

You don't know my character yet. When one puts a yoke on my contrary disposition, constraint only wakens my desires. I have lived in the world in the midst of pleasure. Presently, Worthy is ready to marry me. Many wild ideas pass through my head. I have the heart, the wit, the sense, the right! In short, you will soon see the little traits of my character. But, why is the door open?

Jenny

Fie. Your old Cereberus is on the prowl. What will

he ask? He prowls everywhere. He stands sentinel all Night and at daybreak he goes scouting. If, by good luck, he could be trapped into some ambush, a little spoke put in his wheel, with some compromising story and blackmailed— But, peace, I hear a noise: someone's coming—let's listen.

(Arabella and Jenny draw back as Albert enters.)

Albert

I've circled the house, all night long, and found everybody asleep. This will foil the efforts of my enemies. I've even patrolled outside. Thank heaven, everything is all right. A secret terror disquiets me, despite my efforts. I've seen a certain inquisitive person prowling around here, from a distance, who seems to me to be examining the place. For nearly six months, my cowardly complacence has endangered my prudent action, and to let Arabella breathe easily disquiets my soul, so I must shut her up. You don't make girls wise by softness. I am going to bar the windows with bars as big as my hand to foil all human efforts. But, I hear some noise! I see an object which walks and turns about in the half light. Who goes there...? Nobody answers. This affected silence bodes no good.

Jenny

I tremble.

Albert

It's Jenny. Arabella is with her.

Arabella

So, it's you, sir, playing sentinel?

Albert

Yes, yes, it's me, it's me. But at this time of day, what are you doing in this place, if you please?

Arabella

Neither Jenny nor I sleep in the morning, so we came here to be under the trees and to see the sun rise and take the air.

Jenny (trying to be helpful)

Yes.

Albert

You are to watch the dawn and take the air from your window. You are conspiring here to betray me.

Jenny (aside)

That wouldn't be a bad idea!

Albert

What do you say?

Jenny

Not a word.

Albert

Prudent, circumspect girls who are not up to some intrigue sleep tranquilly in their bed and don't take the air so early be it hot or cold.

Jenny

And how, if you please, do you expect us to rest when all night one hears nothing but coming, going, opening, closing, crying, tossing, scratching, running, sneezing, coughing? When, by great luck, I fall asleep a frightful jangling of keys starts me awake. I try to go back to sleep, but cannot. A Wandering Jew who does evil with the greatest pleasure, a mischievous imp vomited by hell to earth, to make an eternal war with sleeping men begins his uproar and annoys us all.

Albert

And what is this imp and Wandering Jew?

Jenny

You.

Albert

Me?

Jenny

Yes, you. I believe that these rude manners come from some spirit who is in need of prayers. And to better understand whether this angry thing was soul or body, that made this Sabbath, one evening, I took a cord with two ends firmly attached upstairs. It had the effect I hoped. So soon as all were retired to sleep, I waited in person without noise or light, on guard in a corner. I wasn't long waiting. So pitty-pat down the spirit came, noisily tumbling over the cord. He measured the stairs with his nose. Suddenly, I heard him cry: —Help, I am dead.— As these cries increased, at which I laughed very much, I ran and found you spread out with an apostrophe in place of your face. Your nose gave proof that you were a body and not a spirit.

Albert

Ah, miserable scoundrel, adherent of the devil! It was you who played that abominable trick. You wished to kill me with this cursed act!

Jenny (innocently)

No, it was only to trap the ghost.

Albert

I don't know what prevents me from beating you up!

Arabella

Sir, easy.

Albert

You, too, my pretty, could earn some slaps. Shut up, if you please. To punish her audacity, I will drive her from my house. How do you like that?

Jenny (crying)

Just heaven, what a sentence. Sir—

Albert (adamant)

No, out of the nest, if you please.

Jenny (laughing)

Ah, my word, sir, you flatter yourself if you think that leaving your sad company will make me suffer the least pang. A school boy leaving his tutor, a woman a long time celibate who leaves her relatives to get married, a slave who leaves the hands of his masters, an old prisoner who breaks his chains after thirty years, an heir who sees his uncle give up the ghost, a husband when the plague takes his plaguey wife,—doesn't have half the pleasure I take in receiving from you this happy discharge.

Albert

Leaving me would please you?

Jenny

The greatest pleasure I will have in my life.

Albert

Really! If that is so, I've changed my mind. I do not intend to give you this pleasure. You will stay here to do penance. And you will, without arguing, go in, and be diligent.

(Arabella reenters and curtsies. As Jenny starts to go, Albert stops her.)

Albert

You stay—I wish to speak to you without witnesses. (aside) I'll have to butter her up. I need her services. (aloud) Come on—let's make peace and live sensibly. At bottom I love you—and more than you think.

Jenny

And I also love you more than you think.

Albert

A pretty amour, truly to break my nose. But, I pardon all, and promise you that you will enjoy my bounty if you serve me on occasion.

Jenny

Let's see. What service is in question?

Albert

You've known for a long time, that as regards Arabella, I have, as one ought, a soul a bit tender. But for the precautions I take for her the wench would soon take the bit in her teeth. She's always spent her life in high society with the lady from London—Mrs. Worthy—who took care of her until she was fifteen. That lady, having died, a relation begged me to take care of her, and confided her to me. Since then love has stolen into my heart. I have a plan to make her my wife.

Jenny

Your wife! Fie!

Albert

What do you mean by that tone?

Jenny

Fie, I tell you.

Albert

What?

Jenny

Hey, fie! Fie! I tell you. You are too intelligent to commit such a stupidity, and I tell you to your grey beard.

Albert

I never had children by my late wife—and I wish to finish what I've begun to have heirs whose happy birth will ruin the hopes of all my collaterals.

Jenny

My word, sir, make as many as you please. You won't have any posterity left behind, and it is I who tell you so.

Albert

And why is that?

Jenny

How do I know?

Albert

Who has given you the privilege of soothsaying? Say, speak, respond!

Jenny

My God, I said nothing except what's reasonable, and you know it! I understand myself and that's sufficient.

Albert

Don't trouble yourself. It's my business and none of yours!

Jenny

Ah, you're right.

Albert

Look, you know that around here, one cannot take a step without falling into some ambush. The snares that surround my soul alarm me. I have a prize ewe lamb surrounded by care, but the ravishing wolves are prowling in hopes of carrying her off. I must protect her from their cruel fangs, and so as not to fear their cruel fury, I intend to close all parts of the sheep pen, to carefully surround my house with iron bars, and to let in only a few people, and that by day. I have need of your help at this juncture, so that the fencing will go as I intend.

Jenny

Who, me?

Albert

I don't wish this invention to appear to be the result of my precaution. Arabella would be alarmed with reason, to see my care result in her being locked in—that might cause her to become cold to me. But, with clever girls, one must gild the pill adroitly, and make her understand that all that is being done is only to protect her and that last night a number of bandits got into a nearby house and left only the walls standing.

Jenny

But, sir, do you think with this trick and many others of the same type that you employ—do you believe that you will make her love you?

Albert

That's not your worry; suffice that I wish it.

Jenny

Go on, at your age, to wish to taste of marriage a second time. Crazier still, to be amorous of a fifteen year old, and yet crazier to plan to cage her up. I count three extravagances in this plan likely to be funereal in its consequence—and the least of them leads straight to Bedlam.

Albert

I have excellent reasons for my conduct.

Jenny

Thanks to the effects of celestial bounty, I have my virtue intact. But, if I had a husband or a lover of your mind, they'd have horns all over their heads, by God! If you choose me to take on this trouble, I tell you plainly, your hope is vain. I don't intend to meddle in your cowardly plans. The case is too villainous, and I wash my hands of it.

Albert

Do you know that after having employed persuasion, I also know how to employ intimidation?

Jenny

Storm, swear, howl—go into a fit, you will only hear me repeat again, that a jealous man is a frightful thing a thing one would cheerfully see buried a hundred feet underground. There is nothing more hideous, not Satan, Lucifer, and the many other gentleman-inhabitants of hell. They are much more handsome, charming, love-killers—less cruel and less insupportable—than certain jealous creatures such as one sees about here. You understand me. I have spoken and I will retire. Goodbye.

(Exit Jenny.)

Albert

All the world is busy here plotting to betray me. One would conclude they have no greater joy. Jenny's worth nothing, but from fear of worse, I'll keep her. I will not let what people say, or their criticism prevent me from accomplishing the plan my heart is bent on realizing.

(Enter Scratch.)

Scratch (aside)

My master, Mr. Worthy, who is waiting for me at the nearby inn, has sent me on before to sound the terrain.

(seeing Albert) There, I take it, is our man. I must dissemble.

Albert

What are you doing here, by yourself and before my

door?

Scratch

Good day, sir.

Albert (sourly)

Good day.

Scratch

I—are you well?

Albert (grumpily)

Yes.

Scratch

Truly, that rejoices my heart.

Albert

Rejoice or not rejoice, what brings you here? And who are you?

Scratch

I would find it hard to say. I have so many jobs that I might call myself a universal man. I have wandered the universe; the world is my country. From lack of income,

I lived by industry, as many others do. According to the circumstances, sometimes an honest man, sometimes a confidence man. I served unwillingly in the Navy, and realizing my heart inclined to rapine after having spent eighteen months privateering. I carried a musket in Flanders and Germany; I was wounded in the wars with France.

Albert

There are some fine jobs. (aside) From tip to toe, this fellow seems to me to have the air of a rogue. (aloud) What are you doing here? Speak!

Scratch

I will retire.

Albert (holding him)

No, no, you must speak.

Scratch (aside)

I don't know what to say to him.

Albert

You seem to me to have the air of one of those rogues who prowl around to rob houses at night.

Scratch

You don't know me, sir. I have other things on my mind. While Fortune prevents me from having wealth, it has given me marvelous secrets for curing ills. I amuse myself by seeking medicinal herbs around here.

Albert (surprised)

Medicinal herbs?

Scratch

Yes, sir. All my life, I've made a profession of chemistry. As sure as you see me, there are no diseases I cannot cure: stone, coughs, vertigo, hysteria, heart disease, cancer. I've even been accused of using magic. The only thing I lack is a degree to make me the happiest physician living.

Albert

Your clothes are not those of a physician.

Scratch

Clothes don't make the science. And if I were not reduced to be a valet, and if I had not had a fight with the squire of my parish— (mysteriously) But, one day you will see innocence triumph.

Albert

You say you have—?

Scratch

See the slander! One day, finding myself on a long journey, traveling third class, and twilight falling, I saw a certain coach stuck in the mud in a ditch, and a man in need of help. So I approached. And, to ease the weight which oppressed him (the coach was on top of him), I removed the packages he was carrying. The chief of police got mixed up in it, and held me responsible for the lost packages—for an act of charity! That's why my friends advised me to leave the country.

Albert

Always prudent, in cases like that.

Scratch

I went to the wars, where I accomplished miracles. The Ardennes saw me withstand enemy fire. And, battling one day against the enemy, one day all by myself, at Milan—I almost paid with my life. Do you know, sir, I was in Cremona?

Albert

I believe you. But, after all your famous exploits, what do you want from me?

Scratch

What do I want?

Albert (peremptorily)

Yes.

Scratch

Nothing. I believe one doesn't have to have any special reason to take a walk, and doing so offends nobody.

Albert

Yes, but don't stay too long. Your servant, sir.

Scratch

Servant! Before leaving, tell me, if you please, sire, to whom does this country house belong?

Albert

It belongs to its owner.

Scratch

Oh, to be sure. You answer so cleverly, that one cannot abandon your conversation easily. We ought to go to the village together to find a place to stay. We'll be there soon.

Albert

If you hurry.

Scratch (aside)

This chap doesn't like conversation and answers my questions with a single word. (aloud) I will leave after asking the time.

Albert

Your question is funny. You think I'm here like the dial on a clock to display the time to passersby. Go learn it elsewhere. Don't weigh down my ear any longer. Your appearance tires me as much as your conversation. Goodbye. Good day!

(Exit Albert.)

Scratch (alone)

This fellow has quite the aspect of a bear. My word, this beginning bewilders me. The old man appears to me to be a bit subject to anger. To bring everything to fruition we may have to fight. So much the better, that's where I shine, and I love to fence. But, I see my master, Mr. Worthy.

(Enter Worthy.)

Worthy

Well, Scratch, what news? Dear Scratch, did you see the beauty in these parts? Have you seen the tutor and do you see some ray of hope for my love someday?

Scratch

To tell you the truth, it wasn't worth the trouble to race here breathlessly from Milan. You could have spared me the trouble of coming. Oh, that battle on Mount Cenis was no joke. Do you remember how maliciously my cursed mule threw me in a ravine, and I was almost a quarter of an hour rolling to the bottom?

Worthy

Don't jest. Speak in a different way.

Scratch

As you wish, a clearer phrase. I will tell you, sir, that I have seen the jealous one who received me in a manner that makes a cold wind seem mild. We'll need a cannon to take the place.

Worthy

We'll come in the end to what he said and what he did. I won't leave these parts until I am in possession of the object of my vows. Love will vanquish the resistance of this brute.

Scratch

If we had some money for expenses, I'd have hope enough for success. Money is the sinew of love as well as war.

Worthy

Don't worry. Arabella has thirty thousand crowns when she marries. If she had nothing, I would still love her a hundred times better than a rich girl with money enough to turn your head. From her earliest years, raised by my mother, her image has been graven in my heart and nothing can efface it. Our two hearts, which seem made for each other, first tasted this happy news just before my mother died. Because of this disaster, Albert, this old jealous fool that hell should confound, separated her from me, with the consent of Arabella's relatives. I didn't know him, and she, I believe, like me, had never heard of his name. People told me that he was a very troubled spirit—defiant, hard, brutal.

Scratch

They told you right. We must learn, first off, if we can introduce ourselves into this fortress by cleverness or must use force—whether it is better to make an open siege or form plans for a blockade.

Worthy

You always employ military terms. You've been to the wars.

Scratch

In all affairs, the mind must always be used before resorting to brute force. Today's not the first time I've seen combat. I deserted twice from the militia. When one intends, you see, for a siege to succeed, one must prevent anything from entering, know the surroundings, learn its weaknesses and its strengths. When one is well informed about what's happening, one digs a trench, bombards the place, overthrows a rampart, makes a breach, advances in good order, and gives the assault. One strangles, massacres, kills, steals, and pillages. It's almost the same when one takes a young woman. Right, sir?

Worthy

In this matter, Jenny, the maid, is in our interests.

Scratch

So much the better. The more intelligence one has of the city, the more hope one has of success. One must take it Noiselessly, without drums. All night help comes. Make her signals, so she'll understand.

Worthy

Come, let's discover ways to take it. And, so as not to arouse suspicions, let's avoid remaining around here too long.

Scratch

As chief engineer and master of artillery, I am going to see where I ought to place my batteries, to punch a hole in Albert and oblige him to surrender the place quickly or withstand our assault.

CURTAIN

ACT II

Scene: same as Act I, later that day.

Albert (alone)

A secret confided, said an excellent man who's name and country, I am ignorant of, is the thing which ought to be most carefully watched, and in these times, the most difficult to protect. Now, while I don't wish to argue with this facile philosopher, guarding a young girl is much more difficult. I made the locksmith enter through the garden, he must be promptly employed in my plan. I intend to make Arabella and Jenny go out, from fear this would move their hearts and overwhelm them. I've got to call them, so that the workman can act at leisure. When I've satisfied my prudence in this matter, they will have to resolve to be patient. Hola! Someone! Come under these thick trees and take the air with me for several minutes.

(Enter Jenny and Arabella.)

Jenny

Here's unseasonable fruit. What favorable demon causes you to greet her so softly and your humor to be so tractable? By your astonishing command, we can go out today for the first time in six months.

Albert

We have to change places sometimes. Sometimes, in life, the most charming resort bores us.

Arabella

If I'm with you, regardless of the climate, the air will be no softer or better for me. I don't know why, but now I sigh when I am near you; I cannot breathe.

Albert

My heart swoons with pleasure at such talk. You need a husband to calm these sighs.

Arabella

Girls dissimulate often enough, and pretend to scruples at the name of a husband, masking their true desires, often saying they love no one except the convent. As for me, the power of truth presses me and I can find in it neither crime nor weakness. I have a sincere heart, and I tell you, without pretence, that I want to be married, and sooner than later.

Jenny

Well said. What's the use, in the spring of youth, to wish to escape the yoke of marriage, and to leave the number of the living? There were husbands long before convents, and I hold the role of spouse is the most ancient, and the most currently fashionable and used, and the most to be followed in all methods. That's what I say!

Albert

You both speak in the same spirit, and my views conform to yours. I intend to marry. Rich as I am, they're always proposing a suitable and advantageous match for me, but I always reply that another love holds me, and that my heart prepossessed by your rare beauty sighs for you alone, and that on your side, you adore only me.

Arabella

How's that?

Albert

Yes, sweetie, I have declared the love which possesses me for you.

Arabella

What did you say, if you please?

Albert

That, at the bottom of your heart, you nourish a sincere passion for me.

Arabella

Where's your discretion, truly?

Albert

Beautiful Arabella, one cannot be happy and remain silent.

Arabella

You ought not to make such an avowal, and so loud.

Albert

And why not, my child?

Arabella (waspishly)

Because nothing is more false, and one cannot lie with more impudence.

Albert

Then, you don't love me?

Arabella (sweetly)

No, but in recompense, I hate you unto death.

Albert (surprised)

For what?

Arabella

Who knows why? One loves without reason, and without reason, one hates.

Jenny

If the admission is not tender, at least it is sincere.

Albert

After what I have done, basilisk, to please you!

Jenny

Don't get carried away! Observe tranquilly if love has made you a charming object. Your features are worn Away; hers are loveable and fresh. She has a well made wit and you a crabbed temper. She's not sixteen, and you are very old. She bears herself well, and you walk with a cane. She has all her teeth, which makes her pretty, and you have only one. Still, she excites you and you ought to be carried off at the first cough to whatever misfortune down there would please you.

Albert

I've taken useless trouble to please her. I will therefore merit her hate, by God. And to secure her dangerous charms, I am going to lead her to a place far from fops, where by her arrogance, she will have leisure to be penitent. Come quickly, let's go.

Arabella

Where are you going?

Albert

You will know soon enough. March on, no talking. (perceiving Worthy, who has just entered) What an irritating turn of events at this time. To the devil with him and his stupid face.

(Worthy, who was entering like someone out for a stroll, sees Albert and greets him. Scratch enters behind Worthy.)

Albert

Sir, do you wish something from me?

Jenny (low, to Arabella)

It's Worthy.

Arabella (low)

Peace! I see him more clearly than you.

(Worthy continues to bow to Albert.)

Albert

Sir, what's the use of these fine manners? Speak, I am tired of bowing and scraping.

Worthy

A stranger in these parts, and pleased to see you. In paying you my respects, I fulfill my duty. My coach is broken down near your mansion, and after having done my best to repair it, I came to breathe the delicious air, attracted by the freshness.

Albert

You deceive yourself, sir. The air around here is decidedly bad for your health. I owe it to myself to tell you that you will become very ill if you stay here for a long time. It is dangerous and mortal to wayfarers.

Arabella

Alas, nothing is more true. Since I've breathed this air, I languish night and day in a cruel martyrdom.

Scratch

Just give me the same wine as our innkeeper broke open today, and I will stand my ground defying fever, apoplexy, and a hundred years of age to the end of my life.

Worthy (to Arabella)

It's hard to believe that with so much beauty, and such air, that you're not healthy.

Albert

Whether she looks well or ill, find another place to take the air.

Worthy

This object that heaven has taken care in making, this view where my eye is pleased to rest, enchants my sight and never has nature displayed her attentions with so much finery. My heart is in love with what it sees here.

Albert

Yes, the country is beautiful. Everybody says so, but you'll spend the end of your day better elsewhere. By now, your coach must be fixed. There's no need for your presence here. Leave, you ought to be gone already.

Worthy

I will leave momentarily. Tell me, I beg you—

Albert

Since you chatter so emotionally, I am going to listen to you attentively. (to Jenny and Arabella) Go in, go in.

Jenny

Sir—

Albert

Eh! Go in, I tell you.

Worthy

I'd rather retire than be the cause of Madame suffering the least inconvenience on my account.

Arabella

No, sir, stay till tomorrow. Postpone going on your way, and we will put you in good company. The roads are unlucky and filthy.

Albert

So much ceremony! Come, quickly go in.

Jenny

Yes, yes, I'm going in. But, before these gentlemen, I tell you plainly to stop the humiliations you impose on us. We haven't seen even the shadow of a hat for six months in this new fangled cloister. Any man who comes around here is interdicted. Everything in this house is subject to inspection. Sometimes we think the world has come to an end. No one comes here except they be of the female sex. Judge if a girl in this situation has cause to complain.

Albert (putting his hand over her mouth and forcing her inside)

Ah, I will tear out your viper's tongue.

(Exit Jenny and Arabella.)

Albert (aside)

I don't want to go back in so soon. Their complaints and their tears might move me, perhaps. (aloud) What's the problem? Speak! But, above all, be brief.

Worthy

I am truly annoyed that, on account of me, your daughter has received such unworthy treatment.

Albert

What do you mean, my daughter?

Worthy

Is she your wife then?

Albert

She soon will be.

Worthy

My soul is ravished. You couldn't form a better plan. And you do well to get that viper in hand. All husbands ought to do as you do. Women today are such coquettes.

Albert

I intend to rule the roost, and not follow the manners of these times.

Scratch

Oh, may you do better! I am so crazy about women and I am delighted when good souls make use of a little authority from time to time.

Albert (aside)

This boy pleases me; he speaks sensibly.

Worthy

As for me, I see nothing blamable. For a man, without ever being bothered by suspicions, to be lulled by the promise of a woman, to count tranquilly on her frail virtue believing that God has made a woman faithful for him alone, is to be a fool. It's necessary to be watchful at all times. When she scolds, cry louder still and despite all the precautions which love causes a man to take, the more refined he is, the bigger the dupe.

Albert

We are a little devious about these matters which could easily trap me. Each day I invent some crafty way of defeating their trickery and finesse. My word, you'd be wasting your time. Gentlemen, the defenders of women, debonair husbands, soft courtiers, powdered blondes, and all those who are searching the town for a woman whose husband gives them easy access tell everybody I'm a brute, a jealous husband. In the depth of my heart, I laugh at them.

Worthy

Because you are jealous, does that mean you are prevented from having a tender and sensitive heart? Without being a little jealous one cannot be a lover. They say a jealous man who quarrels without cease is more a tyrant than a lover to a beautiful woman. Ceaselessly, agitated by fury or boredom, he takes pleasure in the malady of another. Insupportable to all, odious to himself, everybody to deceive him pretends to be extremely pleased, but wishes that it was permitted to smother him like a raging monster escaped from hell. That's the way one ordinarily speaks in the world. But, for me, I take the contrary position, and say that it's a gallant man who shows so much love through his jealous transports and sees himself come to life when yielding to his penchant. In life, one spices up love with a little jealousy.

Albert

Decidedly, you charm me with your wit, sir. I wish it were all written down to explain to sots who blame my manner.

Scratch

Let us go in, sir. There, to satisfy you, I will write it all down without charge.

Albert (stopping him)

I am much obliged to you. I will remember it well. I believe you have nothing more to say to me. There's your road, sir, good day. I retire. May heaven maintain you in these fine sentiments and not leave you in these parts for very long.

(Enter Jenny.)

Jenny

Help, neighbors! What a terrible accident. What a sad adventure. Ah, heaven, is it possible? The poor Squire Albert—what will become of you? The blow is mortal. I cannot recall it.

Albert

What's happened?

Jenny

The most terrible disgrace.

Albert

But still, it's better to know what has happened.

Jenny

Arabella—

Worthy

Well, Arabella—?

Jenny

In this instant, quiite suddenly, Arabella has gone mad.

Albert

Arabella is crazy?

Worthy

Ah, heaven.

Albert

This is unbelievable.

Jenny

Ah, sir, this misfortune is only too true. When, by your express order, she had vowed to knit, this cursed locksmith came to irritate us. So she vowed that these bars and grills to which the locksmith condemns the window—At the same time, I swear her eyes rolled and her suddenly stricken spirit evaporated. She talks extravagantly. She runs, she creeps, she sings, she dances, she dresses, then she changes her clothes suddenly with whatever happens to be at hand, just now, from your wardrobe, she took your large robe and skull-cap. Then, taking her guitar, she sings different tunes in strange jargon. In fact, she's a hundred times worse than I was able to explain. One can't help crying, and laughing, too.

Worthy

What do I hear? Just heaven.

Albert

What a deadly misfortune.

Jenny (to Albert, accusingly)

You are the sole author of this sad misfortune. That's what comes of shutting a wench up.

Albert

Cursed precaution and unfortunate bars.

Jenny

I intended to shut her in her chamber for a moment. It caused howlings hard to describe. She battered the wall with her head from rage. I said to open everything. No one can stop her. But, I see her coming. Alas, she changes her manner and dress every moment.

(Enter Arabella, dressed as Scaramouche with a guitar.)

Arabella (singing)

All night long,
A mean old tomcat
Sits watching me on the sly.
Oh, he's crazy.
Couldn't he just
Be made to break his neck?

Worthy

In spite of her illness, Scratch—what a—!

Scratch

I love her more this way than another who is quite sane.

Arabella (singing)

Couldn't he just be made to break his neck? (speaking) You're in the same line of work? Musicians, listen: I am as you, a musician. Vain, very spoiled, but I work for very little money. A child of do, re, me, fa, and so on. I'm irritated. From one part of the world to the other, they speak of my talent. In a certain duo which I find excellent, 'cause it's mine. I wish you'd both tell me frankly what you think of it.

Albert (alarmed)

Ah, my dear Jenny! She's lost her reason.

Jenny

Who knows better than I? Didn't I tell you so, didn't I tell you that?

(Arabella sings a little prelude.)

Scratch

I like that, sir. Her madness is a little racy.

Albert (concerned)

Her eyes are troubled, and her face is haggard.

Arabella (presenting her hand to Albert, then roughly pulling it away, while letting Worthy kiss the other)

I love artists! Touch it! Touch it! The tune you will hear is in A minor. It's my favorite. Music is lively, bizarre, petulant, and very enjoyable. The movement is light, new, quick and forceful. It sent me looking, a few days ago to soothe the melancholy humor of a man confined to bed with paralysis for whom I sang a certain dance. Three wise doctors came to his house, the nurse, the patient, and an old apothecary who came to exercise his grave ministry without respect for his profession took me by the hand and danced till dawn.

Scratch (having conceived the idea for Worthy to grab Arabella's hand and dance off with her)

Behold a faculty to dance in the round and exit this street all in step. That'd be nice, sir.

Worthy

What, wretch, you can laugh, seeing her in this frightful disorder?

Arabella

Wait, soft—my musical demon disturbs me, seizes me; I dithyramb. The hairs on my head stand up in horror. Don't bother the God that puts me in this fury. I feel that my excitement will reveal itself in tones. (tossing about and spitting in Albert's face) Pouah! I had a deity in my throat, or rather in the duo which is in question. You will see excitement best, and passion. I succeed better in the one and the other. Here's your part, and you, yours.

(giving a paper with music to Albert and a letter to Worthy, then tosses about and prepares to sing)

Scratch

Let's stand back a bit. I'm afraid of the gods.

Jenny

We'll soon be having a fine chivaree.

Albert

Arabella, my child, your error is extreme. I am Squire Albert, who cherishes you, who loves you—

Arabella

My God, you're going to sing!

Albert

Oh, very well. I will sing, and if it's your wish, I will dance, too.

Worthy (opening his paper)

A letter, Scratch.

Scratch

Ah heaven, what an adventure. The music maestro learns the scale.

Arabella

There, mark your time to take part, you start there. Quickly, come on one, two, three. (beating time on Albert's head and stamping her feet angrily) Go, go, barbaric musician. Ignorant by nature. Leave off baaing. What raucous frog in the midst of his weedy pond gave you your first singing lesson? Do you give a concert or are you braying or croaking?

Albert

I told you already, with no intent to annoy, I do not have the honor to be a musician.

Arabella

Why then, stupid know-nothing, do you come to interrupt a concert when your very presence causes a bad turn of events and discord? Did one ever see a donkey try to play clarinet and mix his songs with those of the tender nightingale? Never did a black crow of ill omen trouble the strains of an agreeable warbler and never in the woods did a sinister owl sing in concert. You are nothing but a sot and never will be anything else in your whole life.

Scratch

My master will sing his part nicely. I am his guarantee.

Arabella

From this night forth, he must demonstrate his knowledge in a serenade. He must make song, quick, lively, and tender which will carry me off!

Jenny (to Scratch)

Do you understand?

Scratch

I begin to understand. It's what they call a fugue.

Arabella

Right.

Scratch

A fugue in music is a powerful morsel which costs a lot. (aside) We don't have much—

Arabella

We will take care of that. Let nothing else concern you.

Worthy

You will see I am a good performer. And I know how to sing like an open book.

Arabella (leaving, singing)

An old tomcat—

Albert

Jenny, follow her. See if it is possible to find some remedy for this terrible misfortune.

Jenny

My poor mistress! Ah, my heart is so overcome. I believe that I am going to become mad, too.

(Arabella exits, followed by Jenny and Albert.)

Worthy (standing aside, opening the letter)

They've gone in. Let's read. .You will be surprised by the part I am taking, but the slavery in which I find myself becomes harder each day, and I believe it permits me to dare anything. You, on your part, try to deliver me from the tyranny of a man I hate as much as I love you.— What do you say, I beg you, about all you've seen of this madness?

Scratch

I admire the resources of feminine wit when it is ignited by the imp of love.

Worthy

Scratch, this night, without more delay, we must devise some brilliant scheme which will allow us to free her from such a hard yoke.

Scratch

You intend to carry her off?

Worthy

That would be the quickest and safest way.

Scratch

Agreed. But, doing you a good turn, I fear that—

Worthy

What do you fear?

Scratch

Justice. The law.

Worthy

We've got to marry her.

Scratch

That's understood. You will be married, and I will be hanged.

Worthy

I've got an idea for a plan; you know Lovelace?

Scratch

Certainly.

Worthy

We can take refuge with such a friend. His country house is not far off. It's with Lovelace, that I intend to choose an exile in leaving these parts. There, braving the scorn and rage of the jealous would-be husband we will prepare, in this place, and we will manage to marry, and make love—

(Enter Albert.)

Albert

Oh, sir, forgive the boredom which possesses me; I came back to find some remedy. This is your man?

Worthy

Yes, he is.

Albert

Please tell him to employ himself in aiding me today.

Worthy

And what can he do for you? Speak!

Albert

He deigned, earlier, to inform me of his medical knowledge. He has a thousand secret cures for many illnesses. Perhaps, he has one for weak-mindedness?

Scratch

Yes, yes, I have more than one of those salutary effects. But you treated me in a manner, rather—

Albert

Ah, sir—

Scratch

To refuse to give a chap the time of day—

Albert

Forgive my error.

Scratch

Nowhere in my life did anyone ever treat me so—not even in Barbary.

Albert (piteously)

Oh, can you see a thing, so charming, put an end to her days, without giving aid? (to Worthy) Sir, speak for me.

Worthy

Scratch, I beg you, try to cure the evil this pretty lady is suffering from.

Scratch

For you, once again, I sacrifice my resentment. Yes, I will cure her and radically.

Albert

What—can you—?

Scratch

Go in. I am going to search my book for the most appropriate cure. You will soon see me in operation.

Albert

I cannot express my feeling of obligation. May it be more safe than my fortune or my life.

(Exit Albert.)

Scratch

Go, I know nothing, and she won't be cured.

Worthy

What made you say that? What happy fate made you become a physician in his eyes?

Scratch

Word of honor, I know nothing about it. What I can tell you, is that as soon as I saw him, after he intercepted me, to disguise my plan and hide myself the better, I told him I was looking for some medicinal herbs hereabouts, and that I had admirable secret cures for all sorts of ills, and, in short, could cure, the incurable. And that's exactly how he made his mistake.

Worthy

We must profit by it now. In my heart, I feel the rebirth of hope and joy. Come, let's consider and see by what means we can succeed in our noble project and bring forth your brilliant medicinal art and secret remedies.

Scratch

Me? I'm ready for anything. But, it's useless to undertake a project without the first ingredient. We have no money. Who will give us any?

Worthy (showing the letter)

Love will provide for us.

Scratch

Love will provide it? It seems as though billet douxs have become bills of exchanges. Strange.

CURTAIN

ACT III

Scene: same as Act II, later that day towards dusk.

Enter Worthy.

Worthy

I keep returning and going over all I intend to do. How can a witty girl, so reasonable and sensible, when love seizes her, be able to display her genius and her passion at the very same time? For my part, I owe it all the consideration love can think of. Scratch is prepared for all he must do. Some help with money will be necessary for us.

(Enter Albert.)

Albert

I cannot stay in this place a single moment. I come, I go, I run about. Everything increases my torment. Near her, my wit is troubled like hers. Her access of madness redoubles every moment. (seeing Worthy) Ah, sir, am I sufficiently numbered amongst those who are considered your friends that I can rely on the aid you have promised me? Will this man who boasted to me of his talents use his experience? In the state I am in, I ought to consent to anything: when one loves completely one takes all risks.

Worthy

I take it as a pleasure to do you this good turn. At all times one ought to do good deeds. Today's patient made me pity her too much for me not to show you signs of friendship. The man in question will be here soon. I wanted to test him and understand his knowledge of this malady. But he spoke to me in terms so precise, explaining to me the cause and effect, that in all truth, I believe he knows more than anyone else.

Albert

Sir, what service can equal yours? Heaven itself, effortlessly, sent this person here expressly to oblige me.

Worthy

I won't guarantee this profound science. You know that these people come from all over like Gypsies, carrying treasured remedies for all sorts of ills. It's much, if they don't claim to have resuscitated the dead; but if one can judge what he can do from what he told me this is the man for your business. He only wants to wait till sundown. If you wish it, you may test him. Thus, I discharge my duty as a friend.

Albert

Sir, I am persuaded of his merit. Everyday we see how this sort of man learns secrets from traveling the world over.

(Enter Jenny.)

Jenny

Ah, heavens! You are indeed going to see another folly; if this lasts long, you'll have to tie her up.

(Enter Arabella, her hair is completely gray, her clothes disheveled.)

Arabella

Good day, sweet friends, God protect ye, my children! Well, what is it? How do you spend your time? May heaven send you health for a long time, and keep you strong and happy. Sorrow's no good and frets the spirit. You have to enjoy yourself, and it's I who say it.

Worthy

In spite of her age, I find her charming. One can still look for the return of youth.

Arabella

Ho! You look at me you are amazed to find me so young with grey hair. I feel better than all of you: I take four meals a day, and I read without glasses. I drink rum, or whatever is available, stale or fresh. I drink it to the last drop and I never mix it with water. I genteelly empty my two bottles.

Jenny

Plague!

Arabella

Yes, truly, some more champagne without any delay. You can see all my teeth in my mouth. Do you see, I'll be ninety-eight come Easter?

Jenny

Her youth is the last straw.

Arabella

There's more still. But I am of a green old age. At the age I'm at, I still don't allow myself any servants, besides, they'd charge me too much. But, do you see, my friend, do you want me to tell you? People today, they're shoddy goods they're not worth anything, and I wouldn't bend over to pick up the lot of them.

Worthy

Is she often overcome with these vapors?

Albert

Alas, never. She must be bewitched.

Arabella

At my age, I am still worth my weight in gold. My children have done me wrong. I don't look half my age. If I hadn't been married at thirteen, to tell you the truth, marriage and childbearing puts an end to youth. Such great peril. I never can remember having been a child. To tell you the truth, I was pretty enough. At twenty-seven I had fourteen children.

Jenny

What fertility! Fourteen!

Arabella

Yes, all swarming. And all boys. I've never had any girls. And you see others turn out like ours. But (winking) they're rogues who'll turn out badly. These evil ones wanted to see me in a hospital. Would you believe that after the death of their late father, they squabbled with me over my dower rights? A dower earned so legitimately.

Albert

Alas, can one push mental aberration further?

Jenny (aside)

My word, the little baggage plays her role charmingly.

Arabella

I will need a hundred crowns. Lend them me, sir, to pay for expenses and to bribe the judge in my unfortunate case.

Albert

You dream, my child, but to satisfy you, I will advance expenses and make your case my business.

Arabella

If I don't have money today, I'll be in despair.

Albert

But think, child—

Arabella

You're an honest man. Don't refuse to give me that sum.

Albert

I intend to humor her.

Worthy

You're wise to do so. You shouldn't contradict her directly.

Jenny

If you resist her, she's the type of girl to go throw herself out the window.

Albert

I agree.

Jenny

I remember that you recently received about a hundred crowns. What risks is there in falling in with her wishes?

Albert

It's true that, right now, I could take them away from her. (to Arabella) Here. Here's the money, go. May these hundred crowns give great success to your law suit.

Arabella

Now I am sure of succeeding in our business. (taking the purse) But this aid was quite necessary. Give my lawyer this money, Jenny. I believe he will be diligent in serving me.

Jenny

He will lack nothing.

Worthy

You may be sure, Madame, that I wish to serve you with all my soul.

Arabella

I will go back and return in more decent clothes to go with you to solicit the judge in this urgent matter and demand justice. Goodbye. May heaven reward you for this service to a widow who is to be pitied, who has many sorrows, who is set on by rogues.

(Exit Arabella.)

Jenny (to Worthy)

Here's something to speed your business, sir.

Worthy

I will take care of the case. I know what to do.

Albert (to Jenny)

Be careful of the money.

Jenny

Don't be concerned. I am sure, body for body, it is in good hands.

(Exit Jenny.)

Albert

You see how this folly grows. Your man doesn't come, and I'm getting worried.

Worthy

I don't know what's keeping him. He ought to be here. But, relax, I see him coming.

(Enter Scratch.)

Albert

Ah! Sir, come. We both await your arrival with impatience.

Scratch

A wise philosopher said elegantly: in all things make haste slowly. I've been doing research for some time to determine if the malady whose remedy we are seeking resides in the upper or lower regions. Hippocrates says yes, but Galen says no. It seems to me, time spent reconciling these gentlemen isn't wasted.

Albert

Have you discovered, sir, from whence her malady proceeds?

Scratch

I've discovered it clear as crystal.

Albert

So much the better. You must know that the beautiful patient is continuously developing some new crisis in her illness. In these remote parts, there are no doctors. This gentleman has counseled me to put her in your hands.

Scratch

Without doubt, she'd be better in his. But, I hope to expend my efforts usefully.

Albert

You have cured these diseases before?

Scratch

Me? Have I cured them? Ah, truly, so I believe. There's a bit of magic in my art. With three words, that I was taught by a Jew in Arabia, I cured a child in the Congo, a kid who really had quite a case of vertigo. I leave it to doctors to practice their science on diseases which pain the body. The object of my specialty is more noble. It cures all ills which attack the mind. I wish you were to become manic now atrabalious, mad, even hypochondriacal. So as to have the pleasure of rendering you as wise as I am by tomorrow and healthy in body, too.

Albert

Sir, I am obliged to you for such great zeal.

Scratch

Without wasting time, let's go to the beautiful patient.

Albert (stopping him)

No, sir, if you please, there's no need. I am going to take the trouble to bring her to you.

(Exit Albert.)

Worthy

Everything's going well. Fortune interests herself in our cause. In your absence Arabella, by means of a beautiful ruse, has figured out how to extract these hundred crowns from Albert.

Scratch (amazed)

How'd she do that?

Worthy

You'll learn everything in time. Now, we must find a way to save Arabella, and be off, without losing a moment. We'll only be able to separate her from this wretch for a single instant. Albert won't leave her, and even follows her about, so we don't know what to do.

Scratch

Rely on me. I'll manage it! You have wit, I am not stupid and the pretended patient understands the merest hint.

Worthy

I am thinking of a way that's very crazy but who cares? The play will be better because it will be stronger. We must convince Albert that with certain words as you already told him you can cure her of this illness, but someone else must take the frenzy. I will offer myself, so as to be ready for all emergencies. Let me alone after that.

Scratch

But, how do you hope to get Arabella to take part in this plan, without knowing about it?

Worthy

I will instruct her in all, I give you my word. But, think only of playing your role well. When Arabella comes back, keep the old man busy to give me time to explain everything to her. A few words are all the instruction she'll need. Albert is late, ah, but I see him leaving the house.

(Enter Albert.)

Albert

God conduct the ship and send it to safe harbor. Oh, gentlemen, her folly increases every moment. A military delusion now torments her. She's turned her ball dress into a uniform, she's taken up armor, a dragoon's helmet and a large scimitar. She speaks only of blood and combat. My money must serve to raise an army. She wants to draft me.

(Enter Jenny and Arabella. Arabella is in a fantastic military outfit.)

Arabella

Death—! Long live war! I cannot remain useless around here. My outfit is ready. Ah, Marquis, it's fortunate I find you in this place. I've come to say goodbye to you. I've found money to finance my campaign and this very night I leave for Germany!

Albert

Heavens what mental aberration!

Arabella

By God, officers are wrong to obtain money from the dirty hands of usurers. Better to intrigue—better to inflate the roster. This fellow (pointing to Albert) loaned me his money. I hold him to be the greatest rogue, the worst Jew, the worst dog that one can find in such affairs. I wish someone would bring me his ears.. Now, I'm ready to go serve the king. Nothing's left to do, except for you to go with me.

Worthy

Wherever you go, I will go. (to Albert) It's prudent to humor her.

Arabella

I quit forever the standard of love. Under its banner, I could go far, someday. I have a thousand endearing qualities—wit, manners. I know the secret of humbling the proudest woman. But for what? What do you want of me? I am not made for women. Glory is what I want. This inhuman Glory, with its brilliant flesh enslaves me. The poor sex can die of love and boredom before I'll do anything for them. No more delay I go where Glory calls. Lead my horse, the time is propitious. Post, run!

Scratch

I won't leave her. I'm ready to follow her into the midst of combat.

(Albert surprises Worthy speaking to Arabella.)

Worthy

I examined her eyes. From what I see, some violent access takes hold of her, and will be followed by drowsiness. Order an armchair brought here quickly.

Arabella

Delay me from reaching the field of battle? From tearing victory from our enemies? Let widows mourn, let lovers cry! Children, follow me, raise your spirits. I see your courage shine in your faces. Let all here feel the horror and the carnage. Fix bayonets! Firmly good. The rogues don't dare face us. Ah cowards, you flee No, no quarter—flee. (faints)

Scratch

In a short while, the blood will flow properly again.

Albert (beside himself)

Her wit's gone, without hope of return.

Scratch

Everything's ready. In my opinion, her illness is nothing more than a repressed humor, an irritated spirit, which is trying to free itself. Some demon of love has seized her mind.

Albert

What, the poor girl is possessed?

Scratch

This violent demon from which we must save her is very strong and could take her from us. If I only had a subject in whom I could make this spirit of madness enter, I could quite answer for it.

Albert

Jenny is a perfect subject. No need to search further. She'll serve our turn.

Jenny

I kiss your hands and give you my word, I'll do no such thing. I am already crazy enough.

Worthy

Hurry up. Her illness augments every minute.

Scratch

Curses. This isn't a child's game. One cannot proceed too carefully. When a demon gets in a man's body, I can get it out easily enough. But, in the body of a female, it's quite another matter.

Worthy

To learn today the extent of his skill, I intend to deliver myself to his care. I begin to doubt the effect. I think he's planning to mock you and me. I intend to embarrass him.

Scratch

Me? I'll show you, and put you in a state where you cannot talk. Put yourself beside her. A knee on the ground, and stay put there. Always keep your gaze fixed on her beautiful eyes your hand joined straight to hers. (to Albert) Do you permit him to give her his hand, so the force of attraction will be very strong?

Albert

Yes, I consent to everything.

Scratch

So much the better. You'll see a surprising effect shortly. (Scratch makes several passes over the lovers with a wand) Microc! Salaam! Hippocrata!

Arabella

Heaven—what heavy cloud is lifting from my eyes?

Worthy

What somber vapor is obscuring things around here?

Arabella

What a calm replacing trouble has come over my spirit.

Worthy

What confused tumult redoubles in my feelings? What profound abyss opens under my feet? What dragon pursues me? Ah, traitor, you will die. I intend to purge the world of a monster like you.

(Worthy chases Albert about, sword in hand.)

Scratch (coming between them)

Ah, sir, avoid his furious rage. Save yourself, save yourself. Let me draw some blood and poison from his side. (holding Worthy) From the violent access with which he's transported, I can see I've given him too strong a dose.

Worthy

I intend to sacrifice him to my just fury.

Scratch

Don't you have some strong liquor or spirits to calm this fury? He's going to escape me.

Albert (drawing his key)

Yes, I have what he needs. Jenny, take my key, go, run upstairs, take the viol—

Jenny

I'm afraid I'm too upset to do it properly. You'd better go instead.

Scratch

Run quickly. Would you let a man who has offered to die for you perish?

Jenny (pushing Albert)

Go, quick! Go now!

Albert

I'LL BE RIGHT BACK!

(Exit Albert. As soon as Albert leaves, everybody stops and there is a moment of absolute quiet.)

Worthy

Don't lose any time. Let's get out of here. Head for the woods. Albert won't know which way love has headed us.

Arabella

I put my life and my fate in your hands.

Scratch

Live, live, Scratch and long live Folly. Let's run cross-country to meet our fate and leave Albert all alone here to pour out his rage.

(Exit Worthy, Arabella, Scratch, and Jenny in a wild burst of speed. After a moment, enter Albert with a phial in his hand.)

Albert

I bring an elixir of astonishing strength. But, I don't see anybody. What suspicion overwhelms me. Jenny! Arabella! Oh, heaven! All is deaf to my cries. What's become of them? What road have they taken? Where to run? Thief—Police! Help! I stagger, I faint, I fall for this feigned folly has seduced me, and I alone have lost my wits today. Here's the ridiculous end of my love. Ah, cursed bottle (throws the phial) and credulous old man. Come, follow their steps, we won't give up. Traitorous ravishers, you will be hanged! And you, deceitful sex, more to be feared than fire, plague, famine, and war. You ought to be cursed by all men. I consign you forever to the devil. Let him take you!

CURTAIN

THE CAT WHO CHANGED INTO A WOMAN
by Eugène Scribe

CAST OF CHARACTERS

Guido, son of a Tireste business man

Marianne, his servant

Minette, his cat

Dig-Dig, an Indian conjuror

THE CAT WHO CHANGED INTO A WOMAN

The stage represents Guido's room. In the back, an alcove with a small raised window between which is a small bed hidden by two curtains. On the left is a table on which is a chest of middling size. Above the table a cage which hangs down from the wall. Two side doors. To the left an entrance door. To the right one that appears to lead into another room.

Marianne, alone, seated near the table and knitting, she holds an enormous white cat on her knees.

MARIANNE:

Our master's not coming back. Since morning he's been running through the whole town of Biberach. He's not found anything, that's certain. Poor Guido! He's the finest young man in all Swabia. A young man so good, so amiable, who had so many friends when he had money! They've all left, and all those who dined with us, all that remains to the house is our cat, this poor Minette who's sleeping on my knees and whom we must part with also. The Governor's cook has already offered me three florins for her which I refused! Her fur alone is worth that. Without counting her character. And yet, I'll be forced to that point, for her best interests, because here, we don't have wherewithal to nourish her. Do you hear, Minette; you aren't to be pitied, it's me! Because cats, they are the passion of aged governesses, and since the death of my husband, I can say, word of an honest woman, you're the only attachment I've allowed myself.

(sings)

Heaven wills it, in its wisdom
That my heart be always attached,
In youth one is tender, and when old age comes
Instead of making love, you love your cat.
Still, the nature of cats is treacherous
They cheat those who cherish them.
Perhaps that's why we love them
It's like a memory of lovers.

(She rises and places the sleeping Minette on the bed, whose curtains are barely half open. The cat is no longer visible to the audience. Knocking outside.)

Ah, my God, it's our Master. Let's not mention the idea of selling Minette to him; he loves her so much and he'd sooner die of hunger.

GUIDO:

(outside) Marianne, Marianne.

MARIANNE:

(going to open) Coming, coming.

GUIDO:

That's fortunate! I thought you, too, Marianne, you were going to leave me at the door.

MARIANNE:

I was afraid of waking Minette.

GUIDO:

(darkly) Poor little thing! She's asleep! She does well, and me, too, I'd do well to sleep, to sleep forever! First of all, he who sleeps dines, that's an economy, and then one has even greater pleasure if it's possible.

MARIANNE:

What's that?

GUIDO:

That of no longer seeing men, and in my misanthropic state, Marianne, I can no longer envisage them.

MARIANNE:

Is it possible! So then you were unable to obtain anything from your father's debtors?

GUIDO:

Ah, indeed, yes! If you'd seen the long faces they pulled on me!

(sings) One couldn't recognize me.
Others had misfortunes
That made them vanish.

MARIANNE:

(sings) You must pursue them anyway
And meet those inveiglers.

GUIDO:

(sings) Impossible, I swear to you. I give it to the cleverest racers
Since they've had misfortunes
All my debtors now have carriages
(speaking) And as for me, I'm on foot
That's how I came to Trieste,
And that's how I'll return.

MARIANNE:

That's indeed the bother of coming to their wretched

country! I ask you, what good did it do you?

GUIDO:

To educate us, Marianne. They say hard times forms youth thus.

MARIANNE:

Yours, up to the present, taught you only folly and—

GUIDO:

And stupidities, you mean, Marianne. Keep on, I'm not getting angry with you. Because I had keen and ardent passions, people thought I was wasting my life and my youth. That's the general opinion, I know. But it's not mine. And opinions are free. First of all at Leipzig where I was regarded as a student, I didn't study, but I read Werther and Doctor Faustus who further added to the exaltation of my ideas; so much for literature! Later, I hurled myself into the Opera at Stuttgart where the prettiest shepherdesses—. You know how they danced!

MARIANNE:

And your gold crowns, too.

GUIDO:

So much for the knowledge of women! At last, here

at Biberach, where I came to gather the debris of our house of business, I discovered intimate friends, who, after having eaten up with me, my paternal inheritance, closed their doors in my face. So much for the study of the human heart. See, Marianne, see what I've learned; of what do you complain?

MARIANNE:

That you do not want to do anything to get out of the situation you are in. Why did you refuse to write to your uncle who lived in this town and was so rich?

GUIDO:

(excitedly) My uncle, Marianne! I forbid you to utter his name before me; it is he, it is this honest merchant who ruined my father with his double accounting. Besides, he would have had trouble replying to me, since he's dead.

MARIANNE:

You should address his supervisor, Mr. Schlagg.

GUIDO:

That crafty individual, was always amusing himself at my expense when I was little. He caught me once, but he'll never catch me again.

MARIANNE:

But at least your young female cousin with whom you were brought up, and who is, they say. very mischievous, very satirical. and yet very good; she would repair he father's wrongs, she would make you propose for her hand, she attempted everything to see you, and you kept refusing.

GUIDO:

And I still refuse.

MARIANNE:

And why, I ask you?

GUIDO:

For two reasons:

the first I already told you: because I'm a misanthrope. And the second—

MARIANNE:

Well?

GUIDO:

I won't tell you.

MARIANNE:

In that case it's the same as if you have only one.

GUIDO:

My second reason is the more powerful; it's that I have a passion in my heart.

MARIANN:

And for whom? Great God! For some young chit!

GUIDO:

(darkly) No.

MARIANNE:

For some widow?

GUIDO:

No.

MARIANNE:

O heaven! It's for some married woman?

GUIDO:

(with effort) No. but you will never discover, neither you nor anyone else. As for me, who am telling you,

I'm not actually sure of knowing it.

MARIANNE:

Then it's something quite terrible?

GUIDO:

So terrible, Marianne, that you see, I'd be in love with you, if that were possible. I'm putting it at its worst so that—there would be nothing after that.

MARIANNE:

What's that mean?

GUIDO:

Let's stop it right there, Marianne. One of two things: either you understand me, and then we've understood each other, or actually, you don't understand me, and we are in agreement, because I don't even understand myself.

MARIANNE:

Ah, my God, my God! You are such a nice young man; must you lose your wits like this?

GUIDO:

(frigidly) I've lost nothing, Marianne. Leave me alone,

let me nourish my dreams and my melancholy.

MARIANNE:

Yes, sir, nourish yourself.

(she takes a basket from the back)

GUIDO:

On that subject, what have you got for lunch?

MARIANNE:

(returning and passing to Guido's left) Alas, I have nothing.

GUIDO:

For the two of us?

MARIANNE:

Yes, sir.

GUIDO:

That suffices, I won't ask you anymore. (sentimentally) Strive only that the best part be for Minette.

MARIANNE:

What, sir—?

GUIDO:

As for me, I have a philosophic idea that sustains me, but she, poor little thing! Busy yourself with her food, that's the essential thing.

MARIANNE:

Yes, sir. (aside) Oh, I can't take it anymore! I'm going to go find the Governor's cook, and sell that poor cat.

(sings)

It's my duty, it must be done
I'm going to conclude the bargain, no going back.
Once we make her live
She can actually make us live in her turn.

GUIDO:

(singing to himself) Yes, that passion, alas, that I'm reproached for
Keeps me from hunger and thirst, that's a lot.
That's all profit. Having nothing in one's pocket
You must be in love. Love takes the place of everything.

MARIANNE:

(aside, singing) It's my duty, it must be done, etc.

GUIDO:

When my soul is delivered to its transports
I will forget everything, and feel each day
That there's a need to live in this world
With a tender heart and a great love.

(Marianne leaves by the door at the rear.)

GUIDO:

(alone) She's gone! She's left me at last; and now that I am alone, shall I state the cause of my trouble? (coming forward as if to speak and then stopping) No, I won't say it. And the object of my passion will always be unaware of it! O Guido, Guido! Consider a bit! A love that you do not dare confess, is it not a criminal love? No, it's not a crime, it's only a passion? And when I say a passion it's not a passion. It's only an idea. and yet I call it an idea because it's necessary to give it a name—because without it, there wouldn't be any. So there you have it, Guido. This is where your hatred of the human race has led you! You've become a maniac, an ideologue, and the only definition you can give yourself is—that it's impossible to be more stupid! Yes, I am, nothing can justify me! And yet, I'm not more stupid than you, O Pygmalion, who adored a statue. Like you, I am experiencing an incomprehensible and disordered love. Like you, I burn, and like you, I burn without hope; but with all the more reason and you said it so well O Doctor Faustus, O my master; if it was possible, if it was reasonable, it would no longer be a passion.

(going to the bed at the back)

She's there. How graceful and sweet she is. Her little head resting on her little paws! Little love.

(sorrowfully)

She's not responding to me? Is she sleeping? Is she dead? Minette, O gods, Minette! no, no—

(passing his hand over her head and her mouth)

She did it like that and like this.
Someone's coming.

(closing the bed curtains)

Gods, if they'd seen me. Then it would no longer be necessary to compromise anymore.

(perceiving Dig-Dig)

A foreigner! What a funny face I and a devilish costume!

DIG-DIG (aside, bowing)

He still seems to me as naive as before, and I think I cannot.— Great, he's alone!

(aloud) Is it not to young Guido that I have the honor to speak?

GUIDO:

To himself. I am that young Guido. But you don't walk in on folks when you don't know them?

DIG-DIG:

(in a honeyed tone) The acquaintance will soon be made, O my son, and you will not repent of my visit. My dress indicates to you that I am not European. I am Indian. In the past, your father had business with the merchants of the India Company, my compatriots, and—

GUIDO:

(aside) I can see what it is: some bills of exchange in arrears.

(aloud) Sir, I've renounced commerce with men and especially with men of commerce. And if there's money to give—

DIG-DIG:

(presenting him with a purse) On the contrary, it's 100 Florins to receive.

GUIDO:

What are you doing me the honor of telling me? Eh, yes, truly—

DIG-DIG:

The person who sent me and who desires to remain unknown is a debtor of your father, an Indian like me.

GUIDO:

So that's the way it is: it's actually money coming to me from the other side of the world. Let's put it in my cash box.

(he puts the purse that Dig-Dig gave him in the little box on the table)

It's not lacking room! Ah, so you are Indian! And how is it you find yourself in Germany, in Swabia?

DIG-DIG:

My son! Man is a traveler. Such, you see me. I was born in the Kingdom of Kashmir. My father, who was a Brahmin of the third class, had placed me in the temple of Kandahar, with the grand guru of Kashmir.

GUIDO:

(with respect) With the Grand Guru? He's seen the

Grand Guru? You've seen the Grand Guru? (he kisses Dig-Dig's sleeve)

DIG-SIG:

Very often, but the love of travel seized me. I've seen France, I've seen Paris.

GUIDO:

Beautiful country for a savant like yourself.

DIG-DIG:

Superb country! Where I would have died of starvation if I hadn't remembered the trickery we possess in our country, and under the name of Dig-Dig, Indian Magician—because in that country all magicians succeed, I had the honor of running all of Paris for the past ten years. At last I came to locate myself permanently in the city where I enjoy a certain consideration. I teach dancing, astronomy, sleight of hand. which doesn't prevent me from delivering myself to my favorite study: the great work of Braahma, the transmission of souls.

GUIDO:

The transmission of souls?

DIG-DIG:

It's one of the Dogmas of our belief; because, no doubt, you know what metempsychosis is?

GUIDO:

By Jove, yes, I do know.

DIG-DIG:

Yes, when our existence ends, according to our virtues and our defects, we obtain as reward the honor of being bears or partridges. Profound dogma! Admirable cult! System as gentle as it is moral. Which makes us love our likes in every animal! I am speaking to you in this way because I think that a lad with a mind like yours must believe in metempsychosis.

GUIDO:

Yes, I believe in it! Certainly! First of all as Doctor Faustus says, I always cite him—"If it's not impossible, it may be."

DIG-DIG:

What, yes, it may be? As for me, I who am talking to you, I recall perfectly having been a camel.

GUIDO:

You were a camel?

DIG-DIG:

For ten years—in Egypt. After that a Giraffe.

GUIDO:

Truly! Well—there's plenty left for you yet.

DIG-DIG:

I don't deny it; but you, just looking at you, I could tell you: you've been a sheep.

GUIDO:

(frigidly) It's possible.

DIG-DIG:

A handsome lamb.

GUIDO:

I believe that well enough. First of all, I love it a lot, which is, perhaps, a vestige of egotism. And then the facility I've always had of letting myself eat the wool on— Ah, my God! When I think about it, since you are so wise, I have a question to ask you, a question on which my whole life's happiness depends.

DIG-DIG:

Speak, my son.

GUIDO:

You must know that I have a charming cat here, a magnificent angora.

DIG-DIG:

I know her.

GUIDO:

(with a fleck of jealousy) What! You know her?

DIG-DIG:

I've often admired her, when Marianne your old governess was carrying her in her arms. I've even spoken with that brave woman several times, and I know more about you than you can imagine.

GUIDO:

Indeed! Tell me what you think of Minette? Who ought she to be?

DIG-DIG:

It's quite easy to see, wit shines in her eyes, grace animates all her motions; I will say to you, my dear fellow, that this envelope hides the most pretty and sarcastic young girl.

GUIDO:

(transported) God! What are you saying to me! Everything's explained now; and the instinct of love is not a chimera. Learn that my heart had guessed her metempsychosis, and that I love that agreeable, gracious young girl. I adore her.

DIG-DIG:

That would be possible!

GUIDO:

And it's all over for young Guido, if you don't show me some way, some secret— There has to be one, o venerable Indian!

DIG-DIG:

(mysteriously) Hush, I don't say no. You actually grasp, I haven't been for the last ten years close to a guru without stealing some of his secrets! And I have an amulet whose virtue is infallible to accomplish the transmigration of souls at will. (he shows Guido a ring)

GUIDO:

Truly!

DIG-DIG:

All you have to do is rub it while pronouncing the name of Brahma three times.

GUIDO:

(excitedly) Ah, my friend, my dear friend If you would like me to give you all that I have, my blood, my life—

DIG-DIG:

I won't hide from you that it's very expensive. These are articles not to be found in commerce and at least 200 florins—

GUIDO:

(going to the coffer) Here, her, there's a hundred already. They won't long remain in the cash box, and for the rest, I'll give you my note.

DIG-DIG:

God! what a head! And what imagination! If this is the way you do business, o my son!

GUIDO:

(taking the ring) She's mine! What joy! (running to the bed where Minette reposes)

DIG-DIG:

Take care, take care, you don't know what you are doing. Perhaps before the end of the day you will repent having made use of this talisman. Think carefully about it, o imprudent young man,

(sings)

Before your voice animates
The creature that charms you
Remember the maxim
That Brahma prescribed us—
This profound maxim
Book three, third verse
"Don't disturb the world
Leave each thing as it is."

(to Guido who escorts him out) Don't disturb anything, I entreat you.

(Exit Dig-Dig)

GUIDO:

Now what was he saying? Don't disturb the world; I don't want to disturb it, on the contrary, I want to put it back the way it was, and that won't take long.

(lovingly)

Minette

(taking the amulet)

Well, it's funny, my heart's beating. You'd say I am afraid.

(approaching the bed and immediately recoiling)

O powerful God of the Ganges
You through whom all is changed
She who I love is there.
Reveal her to my eyes.
Brahma, Brahma, Brahma!

(as he says the words he rubs the amulet, and suddenly the bed curtains open with a drum roll. Guido recoils)

It's she! She's a woman!

MINETTE: (waking up, rubbing her eyes and passing her hand behind her head)

Where am I? What a new day! (sitting up, then rising on her feet) Ah! How I've grown! How far I am from the ground. (she takes a few fearful steps, stopping mid-stage, shaking her head like a cat, then stretching her arms, touching herself, seemingly looking for her fur)

This is singular—vanished.

GUIDO:

(following her motions) I don't dare to approach her; and I don't know how to talk with her! Absolutely the same physiognomy. Yet she's better than before. (calling her like a cat) Pst! Pst! Minette! Minette!

MINETTE:

Who's calling me? It's my master, it's Guido. (she extends her hand to him)

GUIDO:

She hasn't forgotten my name. (taking her hand) Ah, I recognize it! God, how soft it is!

MINETTE:

(looking at him) O prodigy, how like him I walk; how like him I speak; a thousand new feelings are coming together in here (pointing to her head). Heavens! What is this that I feel? How it beats. Guido, Guido. What am I then?

GUIDO:

(admiring her) Something that—there is nothing prettier in the world, a woman, a real woman. At least I think so.

MINETTE:

Me, a woman! What joy!

GUIDO:

Yes, no question. Now that's what I've been asking Heaven for every day. Are we going to be happy together! All that you wish, all that can please you— (seeing that she's looking around) Speak, what do you want? What is the first thing that you want?

MINETTE:

A mirror.

GUIDO:

What! Ah, that's only fair. (going to the table) First, let's put away my precious talisman. (placing it in the box, then getting a small mirror)

MINETTE:

I really want to know Me so much. Well!

GUIDO:

Ah, in the joy of seeing you my

My soul was plunged.

(presenting the mirror to her)

MINETTE:

(with urgency) Quickly, give me that mirror. (looking at herself) God! How changed I am. (making faces) But, all the same, it's not bad.(fearful, looking behind her) But is this me that I perceive? Hardly, hardly, I believe.

GUIDO:

(looking at her) O women! Vanity! With you it begins at birth.

MINETTE:

(still admiring herself) Oh, yes, it's really me. It has to be me. I've never seen my features and yet I recognize them.

(turning to Guido) I'm pretty, right?

GUIDO:

(crossing his arms) She asks that of me. (lovingly) Charming!

MINETTE:

That's the way it seemed to me. But at first glance, I was afraid of being mistaken.

GUIDO:

(looking at her) It must be admitted I've succeeded awfully well. All these charms, they're my work.

MINETTE:

(placing the mirror on the table) So much the better! I thank you for it. But I will ask you, sir, why didn't you make me taller?

GUIDO:

There, that's ambition! Just now, she was no higher than that (placing his hand near the ground) Ambitions of grandeur already!

MINETTE:

No, only like this. (she stands on tiptoe) Only a little, I beg you. What's it cost you?

GUIDO:

I can do no more, These are not works that can be retouched at will.

MINETTE:

Ah, fine! You are not very obliging.

GUIDO:

And you, if you are not satisfied, you are really being difficult.

MINETTE:

(offering him her hand, smiling) Ah, yes, pardon, I am an ingrate.

GUIDO:

Besides, what are you complaining about? Aren't you the same as you were before?

MINETTE:

No. I've never been a woman before. This is the first time for me.

GUIDO:

Bah!

MINETTE:

But in revenge, I've been many other things. (Guido starts) Yes, sir. Don't you remember what you were before?

GUIDO:

Why, damn, I've thought I've always been what I am: a lovable young man.

MINETTE:

Oh, as for me, I wouldn't say that exactly. But I remember myself, with confusion; it was really a long time ago. Yes, I was first of all a little flower of the field, a little marguerite.

GUIDO:

Heavens, a little marguerite, that was sweet, indeed.

MINETTE:

Not very; always exposed to the Sun. How to remain fresh and pretty. So each day I addressed my prayer to Brahma:

(sings)

Change, change me, Brahma!
Brahma!
Brahma replied:
Be satisfied!
He changed me
Into a lark

Suddenly leaving the ground
I took flight in the air.
Imitating the flat notes
Of Nightengales
But one day, in a mirror
Desire made me see
Got me caught in nets
And I said
Change, change me Brahma
Brahma!
What a marvel!
Suddenly Brahma
Who was answering my prayers
Changed me
Into a bee.
Ah, what a happy fate
To gather new booty
Of rose and thyme
Every morning.
But flowers' spring time
Unfortunately have only one season.
In winter I was bored
And I said:
Change, change me, Brahma
Brahma
Yes, I flatter myself
Your heart will hear me.
Suddenly here I was
Merely a cat.
He changed me.

They dote on me.
They cajole me.
With soft bread
And nice milk.
But cat's they say
Are natural felons.
For them, I blushed
And I said:
Change, change me Brahma
Brahma.
My heart demands
This favor.
And suddenly here I am.
Just a woman.
He changed me!

GUIDO:

Someone's coming. No doubt it's my old governess. Don't let her suspect your former condition.

MINETTE:

Don't worry, I am discreet.

GUIDO:

She's discreet, too! If I could make myself so. Hush, here she is.

MARIANNE:

(enters aside) It's over. The bargain is concluded. I've sold her for three Florins. But I'll never have the courage to (aloud) What do I see! A woman around here?

(As Marianne enters Minette paces herself to the right of Guido and tries to hide from the eyes of the governess who goes to the table and picks up the box)

GUIDO:

(low to Minette) Careful, Minette, and let me do it. (aloud) My poor Marianne there you are quite astonished. She—she's the daughter of an old friend of my father's who's just arrived this very moment from England.

(Meanwhile, Marianne places what she bought on to the table.)

MARIANNE (looking at her) From England?

GUIDO:

Yes, a young lady. As she was without asylum. I offered her one. She will lodge with us.

MARIANNE:

With us? (placing her basket down) Ah, indeed! For

goodness sake, here's news.

MINETTE:

(to Guido) She's bringing lunch; it's cream. So much the better.

MARIANNE:

What, master. You, who gave up women—?

GUIDO:

Ah, but this one here. What a difference. She's quite another sort, she's purity, innocence itself.

MARIANNE:

(ironic) And she's coming from England. (she takes the cash box into the next room and then begins to place all that is needed for lunch on the table) I see what it is: the gentleman is weary of my services. It's a young governess that he needs. But seeing her, at the age she is, God knows what people will say. They won't spare you remarks, nor barbs!

GUIDO:

(looking at Minette) As to all that, we don't fear them, and we are here to reply to them, isn't that so, dear friend?

MARIANNE:

(going to him) Dear friend? What do I hear? Would she, by chance, be the passion you wouldn't confess to me this morning?

GUIDO:

Exactly, it is she. (aside) She doesn't know how right she is. (aloud) Yes, my dear Marianne, it's this charming woman, whose gentility, grace, and distinguished manners— Ah, my God, what's she doing? (he has turned and noticed that Minetter has quietly approached the table and dipped her fingers into the cream which she laps up like a cat)

MARIANNE:

Why—what do I see here? O heavens, great is my shock! Sir, will you look at Milady?

MINETTE:

(aside) O gods! How good this cream is!

MARIANNE:

That says it plainly.

GUIDO:

What distraction, my dear. What are you thinking of?

MARIANNE:

Apparently—. It's an English custom.

(Guido gestures for Minette to sit opposite him. He pours her some cream and shows her how to dip her bread in it, which Minette does awkwardly.)

GUIDO:

But what a lunch, Marianne! You, who had no money; how did you do it?

MARIANNE:

(bitterly) How'd I do it! It had to be done in the end. I sold our cat for three Florins.

GUIDO:

For goodness sakes, without consulting me!

MARIANNE:

Ah, indeed, yes. (looking at Minette) Now you have many other things to think about. I sold her to the wife of the governor; a very kind woman who really loves cats.

MINETTE:

(aside, eating) Sell me! That's funny.

MARIANNE:

It's to amuse her son, a young man of eighteen; a very hopeful youth.

MINETTE:

(aside) And to a young man, too. (she dunks her napkin in the cream)

GUIDO:

(gesturing to her) Not like that. (aside) She's not yet used to dining at table. (to Marianne) Well fine,. Since the son of the governor bought her, let him come take her (aside) if he can recognize her.

MARIANNE:

(to herself) And I thought this would desolate him! What insensitivity! But where is that little Minette? She always comes to me right away. (calling) Minette! Minette!

MINETTE:

(rising excitedly) Here I am.

MARAIANNE:

(turning) What is it?

GUIDO:

(who's made her sit down and gestured to her) I said that I saw her here.

MARIANNE:

Perhaps in my work basket.

GUIDO:

(resuming his lunch) Yes, keep looking.

(Marianne picks up her work basket and a ball of thread escapes from it as she does so. Minette, seeing it, leaps from the table, running silently after the ball, which unwinds almost completely as she plays with it as cats do.)

MARIANNE:

Well! Well! What kind of manners are these?

GUIDO:

(rising) Come on. Here's another entanglement indeed.

MARIANNE:

(snatching the balls from Minette) Would you please stop, Miss!

GUIDO:

(to Minette) My dear friend.

MINETTE:

(stamping her foot) She always vexes me; she deprives me of all of my pleasures.

GUIDO:

(to Marianne) It's true, too. Let her do it.

MARIANNE:

(pointing to the tangled threads) Let her do it! Look at that! Find a match in that!

GUIDO:

Eh, why do you want me to meddle in that; does it concern me?

MINETTE:

(who's approached the bird cage, playing with the birds) Ah, how nice!

(She upsets the cage which falls on the table)

MARIANNE:

(shouting and going to pick up the cage) Mercy! My green canaries!

MINETTE:

Ah, actually, this is boring! I cannot amuse myself when she's here.

MARIANNE:

(enraged) A little girl of fifteen who has no experience—

MINETTE:

(mimicking her) An old bat of sixty who has a bit too much

MARIANNE:

(exasperated) Ah, this is too much!

(sings) A new martyrdom each moment.
We've got to get out of here.
It's not to be borne.
And rather than suffer it
I prefer to die.

MINETTE:

It's not to be borne
And I don't know how to suffer it.
You can get out of here.
It's not to be borne.
And rather than suffer it
I would prefer to die.

GUIDO:

It's not to be born
A new martyrdom each moment
We can never get out of here.
It's not to be borne.
Silence! Will you stop!
Ah, this could cause me to die!

MARIANNE:

Why, you see then what a nasty mood— . I cannot bear it; I'm giving in to my fury.

MINETTE:

Why, you see what a nasty mood! Yes, against me I see her fury.

GUIDO:

Come, calm this nasty mood.
And restore me to calm and joy.

(Marianne exits in a rage going into the room at the right).

GUIDO:

(aside) Nice beginning! Come on, here we are in a quarrel already. (sitting near the table)

MINETTE:

(with an air of triumph) She's going distracted. So much the better; we'll be calm for now, at least until she returns. (to Guido) Well? you seem annoyed.

GUIDO:

Come here, Minette, come here, Mamzelle. (Minette approaches) What were you doing? Why did you touch those green canaries? That woman loves canaries.

MINETTE:

So! She's difficult to live with. (in a caressing tone) And I am sure you wouldn't want to refuse me the first favor that I ask of you. (she takes his hand)

GUIDO:

(aside) That's the thing, velvet paws!

MINETTE:

Guido, my friend, my good friend, tell her to get out!

GUIDO:

To get out! That good Marianne who raised you.

MINETTE:

I'll always love her—but at a distance, a great distance.

(she passes his hand several times above her ear)

GUIDO:

(aside) Come on, we are going to have a storm. (with an angry air) Minette, you haven't considered what you are asking for.

MINETTE:

(cajoling, with her hand) My friend.

GUIDO:

(with dignity) Minette, you are causing me pain.

MINETTE:

You are refusing me; go away, I don't love you anymore.

(she scratches him.)

GUIDO:

Ouch! God! what a way to be treated. (aside) and indeed she's kept singular manners! Above all I must teach her morals, or at least make her clip her nails. (aloud) My dear, you hurt me.

MINETTE:

(distancing herself) Leave me alone, sir, don't speak to me anymore, since you are so ungrateful for the tenderness I have for you.

GUIDO:

(shaking his head, touching the scratch) Ah, your tenderness.

MINETTE:

What, sir, do you doubt it? That's frightful.

(sings)

Yes, when I think of caresses
That I used to lavish on you
Ah, I blush for it! Because my tenderness
Had already preceded your kindnesses
It was instinct, like me, today
To undergo its metamorphosis
And now, it's from love.

GUIDO:

God! If I trusted myself after such an admission. (resuming coldly) Excuse me, Minette, I want to believe that you love me; I need to believe it, but that's not all. I cannot accept things from my cat that I could not accept from my wife; and if, with this charming face, you've retained the tastes and inclinations of your former "condition"— . I've already noticed just now, a certain "looseness" in your manners.

MINETTE:

He's not satisfied even yet! Well! I promise you to watch myself, and to vanquish nature which displeases you.

GUIDO:

(on his knees) And as for me, I promise in return to love only you, and henceforth to have no will except yours and to—

MINETTE: (ear on the alert)

Shush!

GUIDO:

Huh?

MINETTE:

Don't you hear a lot of noise?

GUIDO:

What's it matter? (continuing) Dream then how happy we'll be to be ceaselessly concerned with each other.

MINETTE:

(paying no attention to him, listening) It's one of 'em!

GUIDO:

And when I depict my love to you, my emotion, what pleasure you'll have to hear me tell you—

MINETTE:

(advancing quietly on tip-toe) Shut up, shut up.

GUIDO:

Well! Where the heck are you going?

MINETTE:

Absolutely, it's one of them. Can't you hear?

GUIDO:

What do you mean: it's one of them? (Minette advances

with measured steps toward the armoire on the left, then rushes suddenly like a cat) What is it? Minette, will you cut it out?

MINETTE:

There, you're the one who frightened it; she got away; this is unsupportable, it's so nice!

GUIDO:

There's no way to be alone with her: you think you are alone and there's company in the armoire. (aloud) Minette, Minette! Here, right away.

(sing) I don't want to seem capricious.

MINETTE:

And as for me, I want more careful attention. I want my wishes to be obeyed.

GUIDO:

What! You want! and I am listening to you! What change has come over your soul! You were submissive and full of joy. Yesterday, you didn't have any will.

MINETTE:

Yes, but today I'm a woman.

GUIDO:

Well, that's where I've got you. If you're a woman, all the more reason not to have such distractions. You don't run after people like that, it's not suitable. With manners like these, Minette, I will never be able to present you in society; and when I go out, I'll be forced to leave you here in penitence.

MINETTE:

Well, for goodness sake! Fine pleasure to be a woman to be enslaved! In that case, I've lost by the change. Before I was free, I could come and go without permission, and I intend for it to be always thus.

GUIDO:

And what will become of my dignity of Master?

MINETTE:

It will become whatever it can. I am going to defend my rights. And to begin with, sir, I intend to leave here immediately.

GUIDO:

(very excited) And as for me, I do not wish it. What are these rebellious ideas anyway? (he makes her pass to his right) (sings) I cannot accede to your wishes.

MINETTE:

(singing back) I have one more.
All that is is to leave.
And I'm making my departure.

(going to the door)

GUIDO:

(running to the door)

(singing) And as for me, I'm taking the keys

(locking the door)

This is my house! I am master.
The door is locked.

MINETTE:

(sings) Oh, I see that.

(aside, looking out the window)

But the window remains to me.
There at least, I will be free.

GUIDO:

(aside) I'm upset to be so strict.

But if my orders are defied.
I get mad.

(aloud)

What, Minette, you would escape.

MINETTE:

Yes, sir, your strict orders
I am defying.
Goodbye. I'm returning to my homeland.
Follow me if you can.

(Minette leaps to the bed then through the open window reaching the roof. She vanishes. The orchestra plays very loud at first, then diminishes, as she gets further and further away.)

GUIDO:

(alone, rushing to the window and speaking repeatedly)

Minette, Minette! Have you ever seen a head like that? How to follow her? I'm not used to traveling like that? Ah, quick, let's take a look from the terrace and see if there's a way to catch her! Gods! Poor Minette! (he leaves by the left, and almost simultaneously Minette pokes her head in the window and scrambles in.)

MINETTE:

Yes, run after me if you can! So long as he doesn't hurt himself. Oh, I am sure he won't get far. Ah, my God! It's my enemy, it's the old woman.

MARIANNE:

(with a cold, harsh tone) Monsieur is not here?

MINETTE:

(looking at the roof) No, he went to take the air.

MARIANNE:

I'm annoyed about that: I was coming to ask him for my wages, because one of us must leave here.

MINETTE:

(coldly) That's already decided. I'm staying.

MARIANNE:

Is it possible?

MINETTE:

And you too, old woman, I've decided it.

MARIANNE:

Old woman! old woman! To hear myself treated like this. I'm going to find my things and I won't stay in this house a second longer. I shall request nothing, for I've found my poor Minette, my sole consolation.

MINETTE:

You've found her!

MARIANNE:

Yes, Miss, upstairs in an armoire, and I don't know who it was took the liberty of locking her in and depriving her of her freedom.

MINETTE:

It's really a question of that; where is she?

MARIANNE:

(pointing to the room at the right) She's there—in safety.

MINETTE:

I don't want her to appear.

MARIANNE:

You don't want! Know that I am here to protect her!

MINETTE:

That's not so at all! To obey me, and I have only one word to say.

MARIANNE:

Me! Abandon my darling Minette. (Minette whispers in her ear.) Heavens! Can it be! (respectfully) What! It's you! It's you.

MINETTE:

(watching to see if Guido's coming) Will you be silent!

(low) Eh, yes, truly, solitude, chagrin, Germanic exaltation have turned the head of this poor Guido. Because my dear cousin is half mad.

MARIANNE:

He pretends he's a misanthrope and a romantic.

MINETTE:

That's what I was trying to say.

MARIANNE:

But he has such a good heart.

MINETTE: My father, to repair the harm he still reproached himself for, begged me as he was dying, to marry Guido, if possible; but Guido wouldn't see me, and that was most humiliating. He only loved his darling Minette. He needed a good correction and that won't be long coming, I hope—especially if you wish to second me.

MARIANNE:

Yes, I wish to. Speak, order, what must I do?

MINETTE:

Hide Minette very quickly. Make her vanish because if he sees her all will be lost.

MARIANNE:

(ready to leave by the right) I'm going to take her out of the house.

MINETTE:

Not right now, I hear Guido returning.

MARIANNE:

Don't worry, I know where to hide her, and soon I'll take her away right in front of him without his noticing a thing.

(Marianne leaves by the door at the right, and at the same moment Guido enters by the door at the left, and Minette hides behind the drapes at the back of the stage.)

GUIDO:

(thinking himself alone) To the devil with travels! I wanted to put my foot on the roof, but I found myself at the intersection of two gutters; fortunately I wasn't carried away by the torrent, but for that, your servant. (Guido hurls himself into a chair) But poor Minette; I didn't even see her; where is she now.

MINETTE:

(coming to him softly and leaning against his knees) Here I am.

GUIDO:

It's Minette; she's come back. Poor little Minette! Poor

little cat! Weren't you cold?

MINETTE:

A little.

GUIDO:

(taking her hands and warming them) That'll teach you to leave me, Mamzelle, to run all over creation. Fie, how villainous that is.

MINETTE:

(purring like a cat being stroked) You're not mad at me anymore?

GUIDO:

(rising) Perhaps, we'll see. What brought you back?

MINETTE:

I wanted to say my goodbyes before leaving you forever.

GUIDO:

Leaving me forever! You still want to leave me?

MINETTE:

For your happiness, because I feel I'm making you unhappy. Our characters are so different.

GUIDO:

For certain; as yet there's no compatibility of moods. But that will come.

MINETTE:

Never. You cannot change nature. Imagine, then, sir, that I was a cat, that I am and that these two natures are combined together. That's simply terrible!

(sings)

My first character
And especially my second
Make me very flighty
My vagabond spirit
Cannot remain at home.
One runs intoxicated
After a mistress.
But could you endlessly
Spend your life running after me,
Running after me.
Instinct is my supreme law.
And its rights cannot be denied.
Near you, even at night

At the least noise, twenty times
Boom! You'll see me on the roof
And not even that cloud
Which covers your face,
Sir, in your household—
I see wouldn't—
(smiling) Spend its time running after me,
Running after me.

GUIDO:

(indignant) She still seems to be making fun of me. And to say I cannot live without her.

MINETTE:

Still, you must now, especially as I have a new master.

GUIDO:

What do you mean, a new master?

MINETTE:

Yes, the son of the governor, that young lord with whom Marianne made a deal this morning, for three Florins.

GUIDO:

What's this I'm learning? And you've seen him?

MINETTE:

Right here, just now, he came to look for Minette, and so I told him everything.

GUIDO:

O heavens! What an indiscretion.

MINETTE:

And he said he was going to claim me.

GUIDO:

(excitedly) Little do I care:

(sings) I flatter myself I've got the law on my side.
And I will know how to win.
For after all, it's a cat
That he's pretending to buy.
To give him a pretty woman
Would be cheating him.

MINETTE:

(cleverly) Oh, yeah!

(sings)

Despite that deception
I think that the gentleman

Loves her.

All the more, because of it.

(speaking) Besides, he's not bad looking this young man, a naive air, German naivety; and with such a master, I will be the mistress, while with you, it wouldn't be so easy: you've got wits.

GUIDO:

Me! How can you say such a thing!

MINETTE:

And besides, he's much richer than you. He will give me a fine palace, beautiful gowns, magnificent jewelry.

GUIDO:

(jealous) Is it possible? And the gratitude you owe my love, my kindness?

MINETTE:

(maliciously) I'm desolated to be ungrateful, but it's not my fault. It's nature, and we are agreed that you cannot change it.

GUIDO:

Yes, but without warning me—

MINETTE:

It's nature.

GUIDO:

To reveal yourself so perfidious!

MINETTE:

Nature.

GUIDO:

So capricious!

MINETTE:

Actually, that's the worst example, because men—

GUIDO:

(beside himself) Go, at last I am learning to know you. And your species is not worth more than the human species.

MINETTE:

(with joy) Ah! Finally, we are there at last. What! I no longer seem pretty to you now?

GUIDO:

On the contrary, that's what enrages me, but looking at your pretty features, I will always think there's a cat underneath 'em, and I see, all too well, that absent a miracle, I will be unhappy all my life. But, you, too, it's in vain that you hope to meet this rival. You will stay here despite yourself.

MINETTE:

(looking toward the window) You know quite well that whenever I choose—

GUIDO:

Yes, but this time I'll put things in good order. (going to take her hand. Noticing Marianne who comes in with a box under her amr) Marianne! Marianne!

MARIANNE:

Well! Well! What is it then?

GUIDO:

(holding Minetee's hand) Lock that window! (pointing to the back) And hurry up when I order you.

MARIANNE: (placing her box on the table)

Don'y get upset, we're going there.

MINETTE And as for me, Marianne, I forbid you.

(Mariamme stops in her tracks)

GUIDO:

Well, she's taking a rest en route. What's it mean? Answer!

MINETTE:

I forbid her to answer and, for greater security, I take her speech from her. (Marianne opens her mouth and no words come out.)

GUIDO:

O heaven, she's mute! Yet another change more inconceivable perhaps than all the others. It's over. I'm no longer master in my home. Oh, you were right, Indian, when you told me this morning: "Don't upset the world!" He told me twice, brave Indian. (Dig-Dig enters and gestures to Minette, resuming his gravity once Guido notices him) Ah, Lord Dig-Dig! (going to him) You're the only one who can help me; I place myself in your hands. Take her; take her away, so I no longer hear talk of her.

(Dig-Dig takes a step)

MINETTE:

(extending his hand toward her) Indian, I order you to remain where you are without being able to take a step, or utter a single word.

(Dig-Dig becomes motionless and opens his mouth several times but is unable to speak)

GUIDO:

And him, too! There he is changed into a grotesque!

MINETTE:

I had no great difficulty, and you yourself, if you say a word I will make you assume the shape I abandoned this morning.

GUIDO:

(indignant) Me, humbled to this degree! I won't leave her audacity unpunished. (looking at the box) God! My talisman, I was forgetting that! O Brahma, excellent Brahma, the first thing I asked of you was a stupidity, and perhaps, without reproaching you for it, you made a gaff in granting it to me. But let's not speak of it anymore. Punish her ingratitude, return her to her original shape. (going to the box and opening it) And by the power of this talisman—(looking in the box) What do I see? (as he opens the box a fat white cat leaps out and jumps to the ground)

Dig-Dig:

The cat, the cat!

MARIANNE:

Minette, Minette!

GUIDO:

(staring at Minette) O heaven! (pointing to the box) What, Madame, you were there and behold, you are here again! What's this mean?

MINETTE:

That we are two—

MARIANNE:

And that she is your cousin.

GUIDO:

(excitedly) My cousin, my little cousin—

MARIANNE:

Who took upon herself the trouble of correcting you, and making fun of you!

GUIDO:

(confused) What! So much kindness!

MINETTE:

(smiling) Yes, sir, these 100 Florins that were brought for you, this talisman you were sold, this metamorphosis that took place before your eyes and so many other incidents that made you go to the devil.

DIG-DIG:

All this was conjured up, laid out, prepared by your servant Dig-Dig. (making conjuring gestures) Who is no other than Anthony Schlagg, former intendant of your uncle.

MARIANNE:

(to Guido) Who must never catch you again.

GUIDO:

And he made me believe he was a camel.

DIG-DIG:

It's you who had the kindness of accepting it.

GUIDO:

He made me accept it. God! Did I believe it! But, it's over and done with. I detest animals, I detest myself, it's you alone that I love. Yes, my little cousin, I feel it now, and if I knew how to repair my mistakes—

MINETTE:

Do as I do, forget them! Thanks to Heaven, I've fulfilled my father's vow, and not without difficulty. Yes, sir, I had quite a formidable rival in your mind, that I no longer fear, for I still have for you Minette's heart and tenderness, without having her character or her claws. (raising her hand to scratch him)

GUIDO:

Okay, okay!

MINETTE:

(smiling) Oh, now you can take it, there's no longer any danger.

(sings) Change, change, change his destiny
Who will.
My fate, here it is,
Fixed forever,

(taking Guido's hand)

Through marriage
And through love.

(to audience)

My faults are so great
I am sure that Brahma
Cannot correct me.
Nor change me.
But if you'd really like it
I know a way
More certain than his
And costs nothing.
Change, change yourself
Into a very indulgent
Audience.
Change, change yourselves
Into a sweet and generous
Audience.

ALL: (in chorus)

Change, change yourselves
Into a sweet and generous
Audience, etc.

CURTAIN

ABOUT THE EDITOR

Frank J. Morlock has written and translated many plays since retiring from the legal profession in 1992. His translations have also appeared on Project Gutenberg, the Alexandre Dumas Père web page, Literature in the Age of Napoléon, Infinite Artistries.com, and Munsey's (formerly Blackmask). In 2006 he received an award from the North American Jules Verne Society for his translations of Verne's plays. He lives and works in México.

www.ingramcontent.com/pod-product-compliance
Lightning Source LLC
LaVergne TN
LVHW040115080426
835507LV00039B/277